Composing Ourselves:

Writing from the Composition Program at Missouri State University

Edited by Lanette Cadle and Lori Feyh
Missouri State University

QVI·SCIT·PERDIT

MISSOVRI
Moon City Press

Layout: Eric Knickerbocker (mrrena.com)
Cover design: Megan M. Keadle and Craig A. Meyer

Library of Congress Cataloging-in-Publication Data

Composing ourselves : writing from the composition program at Missouri State
University / edited by Lanette Cadle and Lori Feyh.

ISBN: 978-0-913785-08-9 (pbk.)

1. College prose, American—Missouri—Springfield. 2. Teachers' writings,
American—Missouri—Springfield. 3. American essays—21st century. 4. Academic
writing. 5. College readers. 6. Missouri State University. I. Cadle, Lanette. II. Feyh,
Lori.

PS683.C6C66 2007
808'.0427—dc22
2007047465

Editorial Team

Table of Contents

Foreword by LORI FEYH   iii

Introduction by LANETTE CADLE   iv

Remembering Nancy Walker

     MICHAEL BURNS—If You Asked Me   2

     MICHAEL BURNS—Spreading the Ashes   4

     MELISSA EVERETT—To The Point   5

     NANCY WALKER—Real Stones and False Beauty   8

Chapter One: Unsourced Academic Writing

     BRANDEE JACOBS—Brazil   13

     NANCY MCMILLION—The Square Root of Two   18

     RACHEL HOOPS—A Turning Point in My Life: My First   23
     Symphony

     ROBERT J. HODAPP—Saying Goodbye to a Father I   26
     Thought I Never Knew

     RYAN EDWARDS—Becoming a Biologist   31

     LERNER KOLB—Sojourn Home: Knocked Up, Not   35
     Knocked Out

Chapter Two: Sourced Academic Writing

     MATTHEW WILSON—The Line that Cripples Society: 40
     Educated vs. Uneducated

     JOE VOE NOSTRAND—In Splinters with Atwood   43

     HOWARD SIMMONS—From the Rack to the Classroom   47

     MELISSA SCOTT—Chocolate is a Girl's Best Friend   53

     JULIE WHITSON—Organic Foods: Should We Abandon or   58
     Embrace Them?

Chapter Three: Longer Sourced Academic Writing

     LEANNE COLAGIO—Social Anxiety Disorder: A Personal   65
     Struggle with Social Situations

     CHRIS WATT—A Child's Need for Universal Healthcare   74

ERIC HARTMAN—American Male Malaise in *Fight Club*   80

SEAN A. WEMPE—*Ein Finsteres Vermächtnis*: The Connection Between 19th Century Colonialism and the Nazi Regime   91

Chapter Four: Writing What We Teach

MASAMITSU MURAKAMI—English and I   100

CRAIG A. MEYER—Finding My Team   103

MEG JOHNSON—Modestly Speaking: Wendy Shalit's "The Future of Modesty"   108

JESSICA GLOVER—A Graduate Assistant's Observations of Popular Culture in the Classroom   113

LANETTE CADLE—Just Being Practical   123

JANE HOOGESTRAAT—Welcome to South Dakota   129

Remembering Nancy Walker: 1935–2006

LORI FEYH is an Instructor in the English Department at Missouri State University who teaches both Writing II: Academic Writing and Life Stages in Literature. She also received her M.A. from (Southwest) Missouri State and was one of many graduate assistants who served under Nancy Walker.

DR. NANCY WALKER DEDICATED HER LIFE'S work to helping students become writers and teachers to become students. We dedicate this book to Nancy and her 26-year legacy as Missouri State University's Director of Freshman Composition as well as decade-long work coordinating the Missouri Writer's Project.

Nancy continues today to teach us to value writing as a way of learning and knowing—both the self and the world. We still hear her reminding us and our students to regularly reflect upon what we find in the world around us and struggle through writing to discover that which is already within us.

She encourages us as teachers to help students see writing as a way of making meaning, to view research as a chance to connect the "expert" outside with the "expert" within, to respect students as equals in our written conversations in the classroom—equals who bring their own knowledge to discussions and assignments—and to always look for what students can do before we search for what they cannot.

Perhaps her work's legacy is best realized when we move from behind our desks, sit beside those we claim to teach, and become again what she extolled us all to be: writers.

Introduction

LANETTE CADLE is an Assistant Professor of English specializing in Rhetoric and Composition at Missouri State University. Her publications include a chapter co-written with Kristine Blair in *Performing Feminist Administration*, a multi-book review of books about girls and digital technologies in the Fall 2007 special issue of *Feminist Collections* on Girls Studies, and poetry featured in *Crab Orchard Review*'s Stage and Screen issue.

THIS BOOK HAD ITS BEGINNINGS as a conference held in April 2007 at Missouri State University. The speakers were, for the most part, people like you—students taking Writing I or Writing II. The Composing Ourselves Conference gave them an opportunity to have the writing they produced in their composition class presented in a professional conference setting: in other words, it was real writing for a real situation. The student and faculty work in this collection is the best of what was presented during that conference. We include it here so that you, a current student in Writing I or Writing II, can see what sort of writing can be produced using a composition assignment when writers make it their own.

As noted in the Foreword, this collection is dedicated to the memory of Nancy Walker, and the first chapter of this book, *Remembering Nancy Walker*, pays homage to that fact. The last piece in the section is one of Nancy Walker's own and is a very good example of a persuasive narrative.

Sometimes students think that academic writing means a disembodied look at a big subject, one too expansive for the personal view. In actuality, most if not all academic writing is inspired by personal interest and knowledge. Imagination is another aspect of academic writing and research, and Walker's essay, "Real Stones and False Beauty" uses the power of a story-like narrative to construct an analysis of this difficult concept of imagination.

The second chapter, *Unsourced Academic Writing*, retains a first-person view while using it to persuade. Although some of the essays in this section are about large, life-changing events, the genre as a whole does not require such things. Some freshmen entering a university straight from high school may feel that their lives haven't had any events large enough to make an "A" paper in this genre and end up telling about a classmate's car crash or when their grandmother died, thinking that big things always mean big insights. That is not necessarily true. Creative writers know that persuasion lies in showing, not telling, so in their view, the tale told is not the point; the point is in what's shown. A persuasive narrative tells a story, but it tells it as a vehicle for the real work, which is an analysis of the event, person, or place in order to express a specific view (a thesis). Read the essays in this section for inspiration, and in your writing try using a very small event or moment that sets off a sequence of events or changes. Taking that approach makes it more likely that you won't get so tangled up in telling the story that you forget to show the analysis and insights.

Chapter Three: Sourced Academic Writing includes writing that uses a minimum number of sources to support a thesis-driven paper. Some of these essays could be called textual analyses, or writings that look at a single source, make a judgment about it, and support that judgment with a combination of quotes, paraphrase, and summary from the source. Other analyses use more than one source to support a thesis, or main idea. The variety in this chapter and the next shows how complex such writing can be; there is no way to learn a single "correct" organizational format for academic writing. Ultimately, there is too much to say and too many ways to go about saying it. It is our hope though, that the papers in this book will show you a variety of ways that undergraduates, graduates, and faculty members have successfully used to express their ideas using sources as support.

As you probably guessed, *Chapter Four: Longer Sourced Academic Writing* is composed of longer papers, mostly ones produced for "Research Paper" assignments. The name is apt, but also reminds me of a class discussion in my first poetry workshop as an undergraduate. The professor was explaining the next assignment, which was a "substantial" poem. He asked what we thought that meant, and I said "a long poem," which made him wince a bit and say, "No, not necessarily longer, but a substantial poem must be more complex." In my mind the two were the same, but I've since found that they are not. Along those lines, the pieces in this section are longer, but they were chosen not for that reason alone, but because they use that additional length to fit in more analysis and sustained thinking. Let that be your goal as well.

Finally, *Chapter Five: Writing What We Teach* showcases writing from graduate teaching assistants and full-time faculty who teach composition as a regular part of their teaching lives. These particular instructors wrote their composition assignments along with their students, and the results are well worth reading as an indication of what can happen when a simple composition assignment is pushed past the basics to become the most it can be. The essays by Masamitsu Murakami, Craig A. Meyer, Lanette Cadle, and Jane Hoogestraat could be called creative non-fiction and are certainly typical of writing that ends up in literary journals. However, these pieces may be creative non-fiction now, but they began as a response to a "Memoir" or "Persuasive Narrative" assignment. Another paper in this chapter is a very good example of a different genre—the I-Search. Jessica Glover's "A Graduate Assistant's Observations of Popular Culture in the Classroom" investigates the research process, and in doing so, develops an analytical view of a slippery topic. Finally, Megan Johnson's "Modestly Speaking: Wendy Shalit's *The Future of Modesty*" shows textual analysis in action.

As you go through your semester in Writing I or Writing II, take the time to refer to these papers and essays as you write. More importantly, go ahead and do so whether or not this book is specifically assigned. Why? These writings can be used as examples to show how different writers approach the same writing tasks that you must now do. As you go over your assignment sheet, analyze the elements your instructor asks for in the assignment and look for those elements in a comparable paper here. Doing that early on in your drafting process will help you try new techniques, and with luck and hard work, lead to better academic writing.

Remembering Nancy Walker

If You Asked Me About Our Friend Nancy

Michael Burns

Michael Burns is a poet and professor of English and Creative Writing at Missouri State. This poem will be published in *ABZ* Magazine in 2008.

I might tell you she's better, that she speaks
sometimes in phrases, and even sentences,
things like I want red cake and I want blue.
Somebody's going to tell Grandmother.
I just don't get that story about the fish.
Next day she says, The Old Man and the Sea.

Other days she doesn't say much, even
with her eyes. What we talk about, if one
could call it talk, are things she keeps trying
to understand: where; why; who?
Let's get this show on the road, she says.
She smiles some secret smile. And lately
This is amazing, but I'm not amused.

One night in the hospital when I wished
for her to die, she could only say
the same words over and over: Save Me.
Can you please save me? I know you will.
From progressive, degenerative, brain disease?
If I were a wind, I tell her, I'd blow right through
this skull of yours, and sweep away the clouds.

I kiss both hands. She's thankful for it.
She's thoughtful when she says, Nancy's gone.
Nancy's not here anymore. Would saving her
mean helping her be dead? No feeding tubes.
No need to force her spoon by little spoon
as if each bite, could heal her—body and mind.

At the rehab center, she says she's scared now
when night comes. She's looked around enough
to know it's a nursing home. To see it straight.
She sits with the weeping edema of her legs
running down, and she smiles a bitter smile.
Reads my eyes. I'm trapped, she says, aren't I?

I push her wheelchair out to their harvest garden:
pumpkins and cornstalks, ghosts, a spider web.
Birds fly over, bright leaves drift, and the wind
lifts her hair that someone has washed this morning.
I say, I was sick, too. I'm sorry I took
so long to come around, but I'm here now.
We sit, comfortable. For a while, we do.

Spreading The Ashes
for my friend N. W., 1935–2006

Michael Burns

Michael Burns is a poet and professor of English and Creative Writing at Missouri State. This poem will be published in *Measure: A Maine of Formal Poetry* in 2008.

I've got this dust of Nancy up my nose
and in my boots, and powdering my hair.
Sit up there, girl. I love the you that goes

on causing trouble. Belt in! Though I suppose
your lid was loose, and no one's left to care
how much of you I've spilled. Straight up my nose

you're captured, inside this thatch that grows
like vines inside a cave, thicker each year.
James River: I love the you that goes

washing with it, the part of you that flows
and won't come back. Someplace not far from here
that Nancy left. You would not praise a nose

sniffling sulfur. I loved the you that goes
disurned by my own fingers, but tell me where
this rage against gets spread. Nobody knows

but me the trail we left. And if it snows
again tonight, how will I find a prayer
to show this ring of ash? One reaps. One sows.
I like this dust of Nancy up my nose.

To The Point:
Notes on Being Nancy Walker's Student

Melissa Everett

Melissa Everett is a public school teacher who was a graduate teaching assistant during Nancy Walker's time at (Southwest) Missouri State.

CLASSES WITH NANCY WALKER meant writing. It was that simple. Or so it seemed at first. I often tell my students, when they sit silent after the first time I have asked for a volunteer to share a piece of writing with the class, that while they may be afraid of looking foolish when reading their work aloud, it pales in comparison to being a college student in the field of English who has to read her work aloud to a class of other college students who share her major and who all have great aptitude and skill in writing. I have had few experiences that fill me with more panic and with more fear of being found a fraud. Nancy Walker refused to allow her students to become too comfortable in the world of academic writing that we all found hard, but safe. She made us write from our own minds, our own experiences. She made us dangle from branches of our own talents, branches we feared to be too weak to hold our weight.

While I gained the critical and invaluable knowledge of the theories and practices of composition and rhetoric in other classes, she provided the equally critical balance that comes from putting myself into the seats of my student writers by allowing for—demanding, really—that I simply write. Time spent in her classes and participating in the Writing Project under her direction are times to which I look nostalgically. Fellow teachers who also participated in the Writing Project often speak of the fact that Nancy Walker helped them remember why they became teachers of English. She allowed us all to be people who write as well as people who teach writing, to express ourselves, to explore and rediscover our abilities, and on occasion, to mess up grandly.

I can still hear her speak the words, her small, square glasses balanced on the end of her nose. The most enduring lesson Dr. Walker taught me was that everything is to the point. During the summer I participated in the Writing Project, she had to remind us of this several times. As we were almost all teachers, we were quite practiced at keeping our students on task and a little too good at redirecting ourselves when we felt we were straying too far from the conversation. It was really the strayings, however, that sparked the most creativity. I remember vividly a conversation about Julie's favorite reading chair and the inordinately large grasshopper she and her family accidentally introduced to the local ecosystem when it stowed away in their camping gear during a family vacation. These discussions became wonderful pieces of writing that make me smile still, some ten years later. I remember explaining that in my adulthood, "I miss having a clothesline like the one I detested having to use when I was a child, but now my neighborhood does not allow them." One of my fellow participants said, "The thing about a clothesline is that seeing other people's underwear flapping in the breeze helps you remember that we are all human." His very apt perspective led me to write a poem I titled "Whirlpool." (The titles "Kenmore" and "Maytag" just did not strike the same tone.) My childhood clothesline or Julie's rogue grasshopper may not seem to the point, but I have come to find that it is the little details that lead to the greater understanding, and so they are the most to-the-point.

Recently, in the high school creative writing course I teach, the conversation was winding its way through many incarnations the way conversations are wont to do. I realized that as each student added to the conversation, it was not mutating into something completely unlike its original form, as it might seem, but that everything contributed to the central point. Andrew's reference to finding out his father was gay, Jason's explanation that all his possessions were still in moving boxes despite the fact that he had moved over two months earlier, Ben's poem about his parents being much older and still as much in love as ever were all really about loss and change. While the course of our conversation had gone a route that would not have been recommended by the fine people at MapQuest or OnStar, it truly was about the journey. Every comment was to the point and was relevant and valuable. One contribution sparked another and another and, eventually, these sparked pieces of writing. Each time I found myself compelled to force the conversation into a direction I felt more educational, I reminded myself that the students' thoughts and insights were all to the point. This allowance for the sharing of perspective will not function well in the teaching of gerund phrases or non-restrictive clauses, but it is critical to the teaching of writing.

Strangely enough, it is most often when I am with my own children, not while in my classroom, that Dr. Walker's words inform my thoughts. When we play vicious games of tic-tac-toe on the backs of receipts while in the waiting room at the orthodontist, listen to *Harry Potter* books over and over again in the van, sometimes taking the long way home just to get to hear the story a little longer, Christmas mornings, birthdays, in all these moments—even the rough ones or the ones that don't seem particularly memorable (no camera needed)—I know that every instant, every second is to the point. The sensations of each gathering evening or early morning, each summer afternoon or white winter night add to experiences that I will attempt to use to create atmospheres in poems and essays or that I will carry with me as memories of times spent with my children.

Teachers of writing expend untold amounts of energy helping their students find inspiration, develop voice, build arguments, conduct research, think critically, write clearly, and become observers, partakers, and communicators. This is fulfilling and exhilarating, but thoroughly exhausting. It was during the time I spent as Nancy Walker's pupil that I learned how important it is for me to make time to write; I learned that it is unfair to myself and to my students for me to allow myself to become a teacher of writing who does not write. Those moments I spend with my family, those moments I steal for my own writing, the big moments, the seemingly small ones—they are all, as Dr. Walker would say, to the point.

Real Stones and False Beauty

Nancy Walker

> Nancy Walker was the Director of Freshman Composition at
> (Southwest) Missouri State for over twenty years. The
> following essay was first published in *South Dakota
> Review*.

THE MUD WAS PERFECT, just creamy enough to look like chocolate to
a four-year-old, crouching in the back yard on a summer day when
the bees buzzed lazily. I dipped one stone in the mud. Carefully.
When the stone was mud-covered, I set it on the bottom porch step.
Then I dipped another. And another. Soon I had a dozen mud-
covered stones. As I dipped the thirteenth, my aunt came out the back
door.

"Auntie, would you like some chocolate candy?" I asked.

"Thank you. I'd love some."

My favorite aunt sat on a porch step, picked up one of the stones,
and put that pretend candy in her mouth. I waited for her to spit out
the stone. She didn't. I cried.

"Auntie, Auntie, that was a mud-covered stone, not candy."

She put her arms around me and said, "Honey, I didn't really eat
the stone, I just pretended."

PRETENDING IS A WONDERFUL childhood occupation. I always have
thought imaginary playmates were a delightful idea. As a child, I
pretended that a rock formation in the mountains was a country inn.
And that was delightful. Such fictions enrich a child's world, help a
child see possibilities.

Adults need to see the danger in pretending with children, though.
Children should be in charge of their fictional worlds, and adults
shouldn't appropriate a child's fictions. My well-meaning aunt should
have made an elaborate show of pretending to pretend to eat the
mud-covered stone. Her realistic act changed the plot of my fiction
and threatened my understanding of pretending. My fantasy truth—
the plot my aunt violated—ended with my knowing all along she was

pretending, ending with our laughing together at a delicious joke. Instead, I cried.

These days, I hear that young people have no "creativity." They don't know how to use their imaginations. Of course, the loss of an active imagination can have many causes. I wonder, though, whether some young people had unfortunate experiences when they were children. Perhaps some children decided that pretending was dangerous because, after all, Auntie could have believed the story was true, could really have eaten the stone. Pretense has its own rules of "truth," rules that are careful about real stones in imaginary gardens.

I wonder about the implications for teaching children to write. We know we want them to brainstorm before they write, to discover what they want to say. Teachers need to be able to ask questions without violating the children's pretending, their plots. Recently, I read a second-grader's story about "The Day I Was Two Inches Tall." When I came to a statement about having to eat "ant stew," I was enchanted. What a wonderful imagination, I thought. Then I read another child's story about the same experience. That child, too, referred to "ant stew." I realize they may have been sitting beside each other as they wrote. Perhaps one of them said, "If I were two inches tall, I'd prob'ly have to eat ant stew." Perhaps the other said, "That's neat. I'll have to eat ant stew, too." On the other hand, the idea for ant stew may have come from the brainstorming session led by the teacher. If so, the teacher may have—unknowingly, of course— tampered with the children's imaginations.

To avoid accidental tampering, teachers could take the children on a guided fantasy, asking them, "Now that you're two inches tall, what do you look like? Where do you live? What do you do for fun? What do you eat?" Students would gather their ideas silently so that each response would be genuinely individual. Of course, even asking the questions imposes the adult's vision of being two inches tall on the children. We probably can't avoid some amount of imposing on them, but we can remember how fragile the childlike imagination is, how devastating too much adult reality can be on that imagination.

The ghost of real stones in imaginary gardens can haunt us when we respond to children's writing, too. That is, we can intrude on children's written stories the way my aunt intruded on my living story. In conferences, listening to children tell us what they want to say and how they want to say it usually is far more helpful than telling them what we want to read.

"FOUR EYES, FOUR EYES, ugly old four eyes." Those strangers were shouting at me. I had wire-rimmed glasses in the days when almost no children wore glasses. I was four years old. I was cross-eyed.

I rushed up the front steps of my grandparents' house, slammed the door, and ran to the room I always stayed in when we visited. I took off my glasses and knuckled away the tears. They wouldn't stop. Then came the chest-quaking sobs that I couldn't stop, either. My aunt came into the room, put her hand lightly on my shoulder, and said, "Nancy Lou, what's the matter?"

I swallowed a sob and said, "They said I'm ugly."

"Who?"

"Those kids outside."

"Well, what do they know? You and I know you're beautiful."

I sobbed harder. Not only was I ugly: my aunt had just lied to me. Eventually, she left. Then came Grandma, then Grandpa, then Mama. All of them assured me I was beautiful.

I knew better.

These days, I wonder about the undoubtedly loving family, telling a cross-eyed child with a fuzzy Toni permanent, "You're beautiful." Even a four-year-old knows what the mirror says. Their pretense was meant to comfort me, of course. Instead, their pretense threatened my understanding of truth.

I wish that they had said, "You're beautiful because your kindness makes me feel good."

"You're beautiful because you make me laugh."

"I like the way you look."

Or something about kinds of physical beauty. Or something.

As children, we were told to tell the truth. "Yes, I peeled the wallpaper in my bedroom." "Yes, I broke the window." Adult exhortations to tell the truth assume, however, that the truth is simple when in fact much truth is complex. Truth about wallpaper and windows is simple. Truths about beauty are not. When adults tell a comforting lie, they confuse children about "truth." I could have told my family, "I thought you said always tell the truth." But I didn't.

Always tell the truth. What does that mean when we respond to children's writing? We shouldn't be like the children who shouted "Ugly old four-eyes," but we shouldn't be like my family, either. My family, by commenting on the value of my kindness or sense of humor, could have helped me move toward a sense of personhood. We, by making careful (and truthful) comments and by asking questions of our writers, can help them develop a sense of authorship. No authors will emerge if we criticize minute problems. No authors will emerge if we blindly praise everything. Lucy Calkins sometimes tells students, "I like the beginning—the ending is less good" (121). That's truth-telling.

Work Cited

Calkins, Lucy McCormick. *The Art of Teaching Writing*. Portsmouth NH: Heinemann, 1986.

Chapter One:
Unsourced Academic Writing

Brazil

Brandee Jacobs

This essay was written as a memoir for Writing I.

WE STEPPED OFF THE LAST PLANE into the small, white, crowded airport at around three in the morning. The flight was long, around forty hours, if you counted the layovers, not to mention the stress our small, senior class had endured as we tried to get to this point. But we were here: after all of the fundraisers, planning, and stressing, we were finally in Teresina, Brazil.

Whether it was the sleep deprivation, the fact that I was in another country, or a combination of both, stepping off the plane had to be one of the most surreal moments of my life. In the back of my mind, I knew everyone was speaking Portuguese, but my exhausted thought processes only recognized it as gibberish, and this realization irritated me a lot more than it should have. These people, the ones who I believed were just trying to annoy me with their mumbling, kept trying to give us instructions on what to do and where to go. They kept rambling directions even though we clearly didn't understand the language. I laughed a little in my mind, thinking about times when I had tried to explain something to someone who didn't speak English. I suddenly realized that slowing down to an insulting pace and throwing in an awkward hand gesture or two doesn't make another language easier to understand. Also, I realized that finishing a sentence with a slow "okay" and shaking your head "yes" does not mean that the person understands what you are saying.

Life got a lot easier when we met up with our interpreter, Egglae. She was a sweet lady, around forty-five years old. She was short and wore glasses, but she looked friendly. I instantly realized she was a motherly woman. She helped us through the rest of the airport and brought us outside to where a bus was waiting for us. It was warm out, and the soft breeze in the still, dark morning was refreshing as we loaded our luggage into the carrier beneath the bus. We all piled in exhausted, falling asleep as we rode to our small motel.

As soon as we entered the building, we were brought to our rooms, down a long, eerie hall. The walls were an odd color of green, and the floor was all cement. There were window-like cutouts in every bathroom that opened into the small hallway, giving off a somewhat odd glow and mist as people showered. Walking into our tiny, empty room was unsettling. I knew that most people in Brazil didn't have accommodations that even began to compare to this; yet, it was more disappointing than any hotel I had ever been to in America. Looking around, we quickly realized that the small beds didn't have comforters, just one white sheet. The showers were simply a spigot on the wall with a smaller wall blocking it off from the toilet and a drain in the middle of the floor. It was uncomfortable, and we all knew that a relaxing three days in Rio De Janeiro was next on our agenda, but for the time being we were here for a purpose. We were going to build a church in a small, poverty-stricken area.

We laid our bags on the cold cement floor and began to unpack, recapping how our flight times and layovers had been so ridiculous and how the airlines never seemed to be on time. We were supposed to be here two days ago, and we were supposed to have a night to sleep before we started building the church. Unfortunately, these were no longer the plans. Apparently missing two days was a big deal, so it was announced that by seven in the morning we were all to be dressed and in the small main room ready to go.

Looking at the clock, I realized it was already 4:30 in the morning and quickly began to run through a list of excuses to get me out of this full day of work with absolutely no sleep. Luckily, my rational side kicked in and reminded me that we were all in this together. Of course, I didn't want to agree with my rational side. I didn't want to be part of the group. I wanted to be the lazy one that had suddenly come down with a twenty-four hour case of the flu lying in bed all day sleeping and watching Portuguese soap operas.

At 6:00 A.M., despite my lazy side, I joined everyone else in the cafeteria, which was actually just a wall with a small home-cooked buffet on it. Here we ate an odd meal involving some form of sweet, mushy fruit and salty scrambled eggs. After breakfast, we boarded the bus and rode to the site. Of course, I cannot adequately explain this ride because I, as well as everyone else on the bus, was fast asleep. Our bus driver, shouting that we had reached our destination, awakened us all, much to our annoyance. We all slowly and thoughtlessly got off the bus as people around us started giving orders.

We silently walked down the narrow hot dirt road, simply taking in everything we were experiencing. We were surrounded by shanties—all small—and made out of the same dull dirt. The doors and windows had no coverings and people were in their barren yards or in their empty homes. The Brazilians who saw us walk by stared, and many smiled politely, knowing what we were there to do. Once we got to the building site in the center of the village, we realized what we were up against. There was nothing but a foundation and four beams at each end that were intended to support the walls. We were instructed to line the bricks up with a small yellow line and use a gritty, thick mortar to stick them in place. We were also supposed to pass out small McDonald's toys, cheap hats, and Beanie Babies to children who came by.

I was skeptical about both of these plans. For one, I believed that any community that would let my less-than-qualified friends and me even to touch building supplies was more than a little questionable. Also, I didn't really believe any kids would show up. I knew that these children weren't American kids, so I didn't expect them to run and hide inside their house if they didn't know people. But I did expect them to be like the young kids I am used to in that if they see someone new, the most interaction I would get would be an uncomfortable stare. And I definitely didn't believe they'd want to talk. I thought any social interaction would simply deliver a scared, shrill shriek and a teary-eyed child running to their angry mother who would give you a look that seemed to say, "Mess with my child again and you'll have a lawsuit on your hands."

Because there were no children when we first started, we all began work on the walls. It was fascinating. The farther I got on my wall the more interesting it became. I saw this as my contribution to the community because the wall had real character. It was somewhat uneven in spots with too much mortar, and it was wavy like the ocean. The interesting thing was that no one seemed to mind, and as the day wore on, kids did begin to show up. They were incredibly friendly. We spent hours passing out toys, playing soccer in the dirt street with the barefoot children, and worshipping with them under an overhang covering the back of a friendly elderly woman's home. The kids were so unique and fun. We named one boy Frankie, and he was obsessed with our cameras. By the end of the trip, we all had more pictures of Frankie than of anything else. And there were three girls who followed me around. They spent close to an hour trying to explain to me that they wanted a small, pink, light-up Barbie necklace like the ones that we had passed out to another group of girls they had seen. The rest of the time they spent teaching me Portuguese, which was apparently very entertaining to them, despite my pathetic best efforts.

We all got back on the bus to leave and slept the whole way back to the motel. We went out to eat at an amazing restaurant, but I somehow felt guilty knowing that those great kids were all eating small, meager meals and going to bed in their hot, dark house.

The next day we watched the bus driver pull into the village. Sadly, none of us were sure of where we were. We heard a small mumble of questions throughout the bus such as, "Are we going a different way?" and "Does anyone remember this?" Finally, the young bus driver broke in—half laughing—and informed us that every single person on the bus had been asleep two minutes after we left the parking lot the day before. We laughed, and then went on in silence until we were allowed to exit the bus.

This day the kids were insistent on bringing some of us over to their houses. We went to many homes, but one stood out. It was really no different than any other house. Same dirt, same inadequate furniture, same humid smell, but this house had one nice thing inside of it. It was a small glass case that seemed like it should be used for something important. But instead of holding some piece of art or jewelry, it simply contained a little elephant Beanie Baby we had given them.

At that moment I realized just how happy someone could be with so little. Here I was, with an entire *box* of Beanie Babies in my basement collecting dust because the fad was over and the excitement had worn away. Yet, here were these people—happy, fun, outgoing people— whose most precious possession seemed to be this small toy from a bunch of lazy, spoiled, American kids who had started out with the mindset that they just had to finish this chore and then would get to spend time in Rio.

We went on to finish the church, and we had so many amazing experiences that it would take twice as much space to recap. We made friends whose language we didn't understand and worked through an exhaustion that none of us were used to. In the end, we went to Rio, but after talking about it, we all agreed we would have rather spent more time with the kids in Teresina. These little kids had taught each of us about something most Americans are not used to—being content with what we have. I realized that striving for that new car or house leaves you empty, and you simply start another meaningless struggle in an attempt to fill what the last one failed to deliver.

The Square Root of Two

Nancy McMillion

> This essay was written as a literacy narrative for Writing II: Academic Writing.

"DON'T*A* FORGET, THE TEST over these chapters will be this*a* Thursday. Review*a* the sections about sub*a*sets and card-*E*-nal numbers. Remember the neg-*A*-tions and symbols off disjun*C*tions and*a* c*O*njunctions." She ends her salutation violently, yet in a friendly manner, shaking her tiny, aged head in a positive affirmation and giggling, "OOO-kay?"

While listening to this longwinded goodbye, I begin shuffling my green *Introduction to Algebraic Structures* text into my all-too-familiar backpack. Probably one of the smallest books I have ever had to buy over the course of seven math classes, I shove it between my tattered folder and red spiral notebook. In the midst of doing so, I look up to the front of the gray, monotone, mini-lecture hall to view the glowing existence of Professor Xiang Ming Yu as she looks to her audience of young escapees.

In gazing at her small, fragile frame and wrinkled visage, a sketch of her vast array of wisdom and a lifetime of laughter, I absorb her radiating energy stemming from her love of mathematics. She belongs to a different world. This is not only a world full of different meanings and mysterious discoveries, but a world I will not be permitted to enjoy for a few more decades. Caught up in this microsecond of admiration of a futuristic world, I cannot help but also reflect upon the past. Even if her childhood took place a hemisphere away, did Professor Yu grow up like me: two adoring parents, a chaotic family, and an unaltered love of learning spanning far beyond numbers and calculations?

EVENINGS DURING MY EARLIEST YEARS as a child were always my favorite. After homemade Mexican cuisine, courtesy of my Hispanic mother, my two older sisters, my big brother, and I would go outside to play on the tire swing my dad assembled and catch lightning bugs as dusk began to settle. Just as the glowing horizon merged with the navy heavens, the four of us would unscrew the gold lids off used *Ball* jars and gallop around the yard shoeless, feeling the warm blades of growth supplying a cushion for our tender soles. With each successful capture came a victorious whoop and holler. But all too soon, my mother's warm accent escaped the crevice of the back door with an invite for a much-needed bath. Knowing it would do us no good to refuse, my siblings and I would grudgingly pace towards the screen door, and, as we passed through this gate to leave a boundless world and enter a cozy shelter, each of us would hand my mother our *Ball* jar still full of the radiant drops. I watched as her tan hand gently placed the containers on the kitchen windowsill, and, though every time it was the same story, I loved to hear her tenderly explain, "Just as the morning sun creeps its way onto the 'sill, the light of the bugs will dim and be captured by a copper shell." As silly as it sounds, for a long time I was convinced that fireflies were magically turned into pennies by the sun.

After my bath, which usually ended with more water on the bathroom tiles than there was in the tub, my dad's nightly ritual included story time for his baby girl. At the beginning stages of this ritual, the books I picked out from the shelf were simple in form, like *Teddy Ruxpin* and similar tales. However, with each passing year my book choices began to graduate in complexity. Instead of choosing *Hop on Pop* or *Frog and Toad*, I started to grab for anything featuring Amelia Bedelia and everything that required an audience with a big imagination.

All too soon my father's responsibility as my storyteller faded away, and I began to tackle the chapter books all by myself. My attention shifted away from Amelia Bedelia, captured now by Beverly Cleary's tales of Ramona and Beezus. After reading my fair share of those sibling disputes, I indulged my imagination and jumped on the *Goosebumps* bandwagon. I took advantage of the way R.L. Stine diminished the known world and heightened the frightening nature of another, highly fanciful realm full of terror and ooze.

My school world quickly caught up to my make-believe world, compelling me to deny cravings for titles like *Night of the Living Dummy* and instead be forced to read books much more suitable for a fourth grade English class. At first, furious at the thought of teachers trying to stifle my imaginative edge, I read my assignment from Mrs. Mencin reluctantly: chapter one of *The Lion, the Witch, and the Wardrobe*. Nearly all school-goers take no delight in homework, and I was no exception. At that moment, my two worlds collided. Being a young kid with no time management skills allowed me to juggle each world separately; I feared I would begin to despise both worlds equally.

Much to my amazement, this new assignment did not even come close to muffling my creativity, but instead made it flourish, allowing me to see how each writer, not just R.L. Stine, could create fanciful dimensions. I slowly began turning my back on *Goosebumps* and began reaching for my new class assignments. One after another, they came like drips from a leaky faucet: *Stuart Little, A Cricket in Times Square, Johnny Tremain, A Wrinkle In Time, The Devil's Arithmetic, Freak the Mighty, Walk Two Moons, Roll of Thunder/Hear My Cry....*

As juvenile as it sounds, entering high school was like voyaging into a new frontier. For nine years, my short life consisted of an average grade of thirty-two at Christ, Prince of Peace Catholic School. Instead of wanting to graduate from a private, single-gendered school, I opted to explore unfamiliar territory. Just as Billy Coleman completed his adventures in coon-hunting, so I could be successful on my new voyage.

So much different from elementary and middle school, every class seemed to have its own unique story. World and American history appeared very complex, oftentimes sprouting characters barbaric and full of pure evil. Dating back to the Conquistadors, flying through the Renaissance, fawning over architectural feats, reliving horrific bloodshed: those historical events fit the plotlines I could read about in novels.

Chemistry and physics class came directly out of a science fiction novel, as each experiment offered a new ending to the story. Dissecting earthworms and freezing flowers with liquid nitrogen became interesting new chapters. However, as much fun as it was to research things like vibrations and naturally occurring elements, the repetition of such a finite ending to the story became boring.

Being a member of a fishbowl in English and literature class became second nature to me. I loved discussing the rhetorical devices and symbolic meaning found in *Anthem*, *The Metamorphosis*, *A Brave New*

World, *The Invisible Man*, and *Hamlet*. Even though I came across novels I absolutely dreaded, like *The Crucible* and *The Scarlet Letter*, I discovered a newfound love of the worlds embedded in other works, like *The Canterbury Tales* and *The Old Man and the Sea*. Except for writing difficult essays and preparing for hard tests, I did not have to work hard to enjoy the classes.

It is difficult to communicate fully why I relished my math classes. On the surface, a simple mathematics course is quite boring and shallow. What did I care about maximizing the income for a privately owned bakery? Why did it matter how many different geometric shapes I could locate in my room? I floated my way through the material in my beginning courses, never really reading between the lines to uncover any deeper meaning.

I became disappointed by high school mathematics. The textbooks we were forced to study resembled nothing like those I read in my other courses; instead, they took the form of manuals, like something one would use if a VCR needed programming. No teacher ever took the time to explain why the square root of two is irrational or the reasoning behind prime numbers. As a result of such a surface reading, the courses were smooth sailing. Just as it was easy to be enthralled by *Alice In Wonderland*, so it was very simple just to memorize and memorize and memorize. I memorized my way through quadratic formulas, but I did not understand them. I drew graphs of trigonometric functions quickly, but I did not know why the curves took unique forms. It seemed like the only thing my math teachers cared about was whether I could differentiate between a coefficient that translates the curve and one that compresses it.

Soon, mathematical operations became mechanical for me. The time I spent on the subject became a break for my brain from any analytical and critical thinking. Although I despised the repetition of it all, I loved the free time acquired after finishing my quick calculations. It was during one such break that I stumbled onto my sister's copy of *The Elegant Universe: Superstrings, Hidden Dimensions, and the Quest for the Ultimate Theory* while rummaging through books in the basement. I was not really familiar with the vastness of astronomy and sciences, so I was enthralled with the extremities of existence the author was theorizing. His creativity sparked past memories. Reflections of magical fireflies zoomed through my head;

the symbolism and metaphor I encountered in stories rose to a new height. Subconsciously, the mother-made fairytales, the love stories, the tragedies and comedies, the thriller sagas, and the adventure books helped me to believe in the incredible and imagine the unthinkable.

Realizing I already had a knack for mathematics, I was not scared to travel this road in future schooling. Though it took a little time to adjust to my new journey, I was quick to realize my passion did not stem from a love of computation, but, more deeply, from my love of finding meaning in the most disparate crevices.

My growth from books helped me to see how everything that has ever spanned the universe has a meaning, and it is up to me to become a part of the search. Anthropologists uncover the import of remains, linguists find links between languages, and psychologists unravel the mysteries buried in the human mind. *How about me?*

AFTER ZIPPING UP MY BOOK BAG and strapping the load on my back, I proceed with the rest of the herd for the door to escape the dim lighting and dreary walls. However, in the midst of our escape to a brighter world, Professor Yu interjects to remind us, "Know how*a* to prove why ir*R*ationul numbas are*a,* ir*R*ational. And*a* why the squewa root of two is*a* ir*R*ational."

Just as Robert M. Pirsig slowly shovels to unearth a definition of quality in *Zen and the Art of Motorcycle Maintenance*, so I will help uncover meaning in mathematical concepts, even in something as small as, say, the square root of two.

A Turning Point in My Life: My First Symphony

Rachel Hoops

This essay was written as a memoir for Writing I.

IT WAS A COLD SATURDAY evening in December, and I was nine years old. Mom, Dad, and I had put on our best clothes—my parents both in black and I in a little red dress. I was going to the symphony with my parents for the first time, and I did not know what to expect. It was novel for me to be able to join my parents for an evening of entertainment, so I was happy and eager for whatever was to come.

My father parked the blue Crown Victoria and as the cold wind whipped our faces, our family of three made our way inside Juanita K. Hammons Hall for the Performing Arts. It was like a warm beacon of light. As soon as I walked into the lobby, I was enveloped by a crowd of fancily dressed, middle-aged patrons. There were no other children in sight; I was the only nine-year-old there. In the beautiful lobby with a giant pearl chandelier, I heard the dull roar of the symphony-goers' chatter. Smiles painted with bright red lipstick and the smell of perfume added to my excitement. I was glad to be a part of such an elegant group of people. I knew something exciting was about to happen, but I had no idea what.

I gave the friendly male usher my ticket and made my way up to the balcony. My parents and I sat in the front. I leaned way over the railing to get a good look at the stage below, the cold metal bar pressed against my waist. What a sight! Several musicians, all dressed in black, filled the stage. I plopped down in my cushioned, spring-loaded seat and beheld the vast array of instruments. The gleam of brass caught my eye, and giant wooden basses stood out to me like elephants. I saw flutes, bassoons, timpani, trumpets, and oboes—all for the first time. My parents had played recordings of classical music since before I could walk. Never before, however, had I seen the instruments that made these glorious sounds in person.

The lights dimmed, and out walked a man with the smallest of stringed wooden instruments—the violin. The rest of the orchestra sat in attention when he walked onto the stage. I turned to my mother and asked in a loud whisper, "Who is that man?" My mother replied, "He is called the concertmaster. He helps the symphony tune." I glanced past my mother at the woman sitting next to her. She was a pinch-faced, elderly woman with a permanent scowl. She put her index finger quickly to her lips as a sign for me to be quiet. Apparently, talking was not allowed.

The concertmaster put his violin beneath his chin and drew out a single pitch—an A—with his bow. After a few seconds of silence, the entire orchestra erupted in response. I was amazed at what command the concertmaster had over the orchestra, and I decided that the violin must be the most important instrument of all. When he was finished tuning, the conductor walked briskly onto the stage with her white baton.

I heard a series of C minor chords: dee dee dee dumm! I immediately recognized the first tune they played. It was Beethoven's Fifth Symphony. I became entranced with the fact that I was actually seeing musicians perform live for the first time. The strains were familiar, yet somehow hearing them in person made them come alive. The music washed over me and captivated me until the very last chord. After the piece was finished, I stood on my feet and clapped with great appreciation. The experience was almost religious.

The minutes passed quickly, and it was already time for intermission. I came back down to the lobby and got a sip of cool water from the drinking fountain. I was contemplating, all the while, how I would become a part of a symphony just like the one in the concert hall. "How do you play an instrument?" I wondered. I wanted to be a part of the action. What could be better than creating that lovely music?

I found my parents in the crowd. We came back up the stairs to see the second half of the program. This time, the music was quite different. The piece was slow and calm. Then, a few measures in, a beautiful, haunting melody floated from the violin section to my ears. Again, I was in awe. After the refrain reiterated a few times, the concertmaster had a solo. His violin sang, and the music soared above the rest of the orchestra. It was as if the whole symphony was supporting his instrument.

I knew, at that moment, the violin was the instrument for me. I wanted to be able to produce those beautiful sounds myself. The violin seemed to be the crowning jewel of the orchestra, with its high-pitched song. I knew then, without ever having touched a violin, that I wanted it to be a part of my life forever. That evening was the beginning of my life-long love affair with that instrument.

The music ended, and I clapped ecstatically for the second time. I left with a thrill in my heart at the new and exciting notion that I might someday be able to play the violin myself. My parents and I bundled up in our coats once more and walked back to our car. All the way home, I bombarded Mom and Dad with questions about playing the violin. Could I play one at the age of nine? How does is work? When could I start?

Luckily at my church the next morning, my parents talked with a violinist who played in all of the morning services. Her name was Pat Lockhart. She was kind and amiable, and she answered all of our questions. As it turned out, nine was a rather late age to start playing violin. Mrs. Lockhart had started at the age of five. She said she was willing to give me lessons, and my parents graciously agreed to let me have them.

I studied violin with Mrs. Lockhart for ten years and came to college as a violin performance major. I have never questioned what I want to do for a career: music has always been my highest priority. The first live symphony concert I attended changed me forever. It is almost hard for me to believe that one night, as a young girl, I made a decision that impacted my entire life.

Saying Goodbye to a Father I Thought I Never Knew

Robert J. Hodapp

This essay was written as a memoir for Writing I.

IT'S BEEN ALMOST TWO YEARS now since my father passed away. At that time, I didn't really know how I would be affected by this moment of despair. I never really had many memories of my father while he was alive. I rarely knew him as a father at all growing up, as he and my mother divorced when I was very young because of his alcohol addiction. Life seemed to work in mysterious ways by preparing me for his untimely death, however: through my own struggles and life experiences, I realized that I knew my father far better than my memories allowed.

The first six years of my life I grew up in the small rural town of St. Clair in southern Minnesota. I lived with my mother, father, and my older sister in a small two bedroom apartment that happened to be located above the local bar. I can only recall two memories of my father during this time. The first was when my family and I would frequently go to the nearby city of Mankato and eat at a pizzeria. I didn't care for eating pizza during this time of my life, so I would just watch the workers as they tossed the dough up in the air, spinning it around and around until it expanded into a large circle. The second memory I have of my father is when my mother sent me down to the bar under our apartment to convince him that dinner was ready and it was time to go home. I remember going down there dressed in my pajamas and seeing my father sitting on a bar stool talking and drinking with the local regulars. As a child, I considered my father as sort of a recluse and shy person; however, being around his friends at the bar you would think he was the most outgoing individual. I would tell him, "Mom says it's time to come upstairs for dinner." His reply was, "Nonsense, I still have time for one more. Come sit down next to me and I'll buy you a soda." Of course, I became the center of conversation until my presence from the regulars wore off. Sometime later, after finishing his beer, we went home where my mother was waiting for us, ready to unleash a fury of hateful words upon my father.

When I was six years old, my mother and father separated and divorced due to my father's continued addiction to alcohol. My sister and I moved away with my mother to live near her parents in Henderson, about forty miles from St. Clair. I never saw or talked to my father much since we moved away, except for when I would visit my grandparents, where my father was living at the time. Many times when we would be at my grandparents' for a holiday, he would just sit in his room listening to Johnny Cash records or tinker with his collection of John Deere memorabilia instead of interacting with the rest of the family. I always felt that my father never really wanted to get to know me or be a part of my life. He never made any attempt to be there for me growing up.

After the death of my grandparents, I attempted to visit with my father, trying to show him that I still wanted to be a part of his life. No matter what I did though, he never wanted to really be a father. I felt that he would always come up with excuses or reasons as to why we could never spend time together.

Upon finishing high school, I soon joined the United States Army and left my home in Minnesota to serve my country. From time to time, I would make it back to my hometown to visit. At first, I would make it a point to visit my father and still try to be a part of his life now that I was an adult. However, my father still never wanted to be a part of my life. My only memories while visiting him were sitting around watching television, talking about his John Deere collection, or dropping him off at the local bar.

As time passed by and I continued my career in the Army, I visited my father less and less, sometimes five or more years would go by. During this time, I married and began a family of my own. My wife also wanted my father to be a part of our family and made numerous attempts to include him in our lives. However, she soon found that he wasn't interested. Once, my family and I stayed at a hotel only two blocks from his home for ten days in hopes that we would be able to spend time together. However of those ten days, we only spent a half a day together. In the end, she too gave up hope of having a relationship with my father.

Throughout my career in the Army, I have found myself moving across the nation and around the world on numerous assignments. In the late 1990s, I was stationed in Germany when I received news that my father's alcoholism had caused cirrhosis of the liver, which forced him to quit drinking for fear of dying. Now that my father was sober, I hoped that he would take an active role to be a part of my life. However, this was not to be.

One of my more recent tours of duty was a thirteen month deployment to Iraq in support of Operation Iraqi Freedom. Prior to deploying, I went back to my hometown to see my father. With the possibility that we may never see each other again, I was hoping to spend some memorable time together. However, I would once again be disappointed by his lack of desire to spend time with me.

During my deployment to Iraq, I was exposed to a reality of hardship and despair. Many of my friends and fellow soldiers were injured or killed. Many times I would wonder why I was so fortunate to make it home when others did not. This experience definitely changed how I see things in life. We always take for granted those who are nearest to us, thinking that they will always be with us for a long time to come.

Upon returning home from Iraq, I went to visit family in Minnesota where we had a welcome back party. My father, however, never attempted to be there. Once again, he didn't make any effort to be a part of my life. I would soon cease to make any attempt to contact my father, concentrating more on my family and where my career was taking me.

Three months later, my unit was tasked with conducting funeral detail for veterans. During this ceremony, we provided a rifle team, pall bearers, bugler, and a flag in honor of the deceased veteran at their burial. For me, it became normal to see deceased persons lying in caskets with the almost daily ceremonies that were conducted. I was in charge of the detail, so it was my responsibility to present the flag to the family of the deceased veteran. With each volley of rounds being fired by the rifle team, I could see the impulsive flinching of the congregation. As the bugler sounded off with Taps, it forced even the strongest willed individuals to fight back tears. Though I didn't know at the time, this life experience was preparing me for the hardship that I would soon have to endure.

After almost a month of conducting funeral detail, I received a call from my sister. She explained to me that my father was having trouble breathing, and that she had to rush him to the hospital. She also stated that because he could no longer breathe on his own, he had to be intubated. Apparently my father had developed partial emphysema due to excessive cigarette smoking. My sister requested that I drive the nine hours to Minnesota to see him. I was reluctant at this point to go there. I thought to myself, "Why? He hasn't been in my life at all and hasn't made any effort to do so. Now that he is in the hospital, I am supposed to be there for him when he was never there for me?" My sister told me that it may become life threatening and that the doctors really wanted me to be there. Reluctantly, I decided to drive up there.

Upon reaching the hospital, I found my father in the Intensive Care Unit, heavily sedated and still intubated. I told him that I was there with him, hoping that he could hear me. As I spoke to him, he attempted to open his eyes and look around the room. I stayed with him in the hospital, talking to him and hoping that he could hear my voice. He had aged so much from the last time I had seen him. His skin had become very thin and wrinkled and his hair had turned gray. My wife and I thought that maybe he would feel better if he could listen to music, so we bought a CD player and a CD of his favorite singer, Johnny Cash. As the days passed, his condition slowly improved and the doctors were able to conduct the tests they were unable to perform in his previous weakened condition. At this point, I had to return to duty at my base, so I said my goodbyes and prayed that he would get well soon.

Shortly upon arriving back home, I received another call from my sister, who was in a frantic state of mind. After I calmed her down, she commenced to explain to me that she received the results of the tests from the doctors. They discovered that my father had cancer in his liver, lungs, and lower vertebrae. She then pleaded with me that I needed to drive back up there immediately because we were going to have to make some hard decisions about our father's state of health.

The next day, my family and I were on the road again driving to Minnesota. Once I reached the hospital, the doctor explained to us my father's current condition and that the chances of him ever reviving and breathing on his own again were extremely small. This was probably the hardest decision that I have ever had to make in my life. Even though my father was never really a part of my life, none of that mattered when confronted with the fact that I had to decide whether or not to remove the machine that was keeping him alive. My sister and I decided, after much discussion, that my father was never going to have a chance at life with his body full of cancer and his lungs not working. We made the difficult decision to remove the breathing machine and let my father be free. We prayed together and then the nurse removed the tube that was breathing for him. We stayed by his side up until the final moments of his life.

During his funeral, I realized just how many friends and family that my father had. People who I never had seen before would come up to me and say how my father would always tell them how proud he was of me. They told me that my sister and I were all he would ever talk about and how he wished he would have been there more for us growing up. At this moment, I understood that my father really did love me, and he was proud of whom I had become.

I have since inherited his collection of John Deere tractors, which allows me to keep a little piece of him near me. Now when I go up to Minnesota, I make the extra effort to visit my father's grave to speak to him. Every time I hear a Johnny Cash song or see some John Deere memorabilia, I always think of my father. In many ways, I never knew my father when he was alive. However through the voices of his friends, I see now that he has always wanted to be my father, he just didn't know how to personally express his feelings to me.

Becoming a Biologist

Ryan Edwards

This literary narrative was written for Writing II: Academic Writing.

AS A BIOLOGY MAJOR at Missouri State University, I am constantly learning new material. There is not a day that goes by where I am not submerging myself in new vocabulary, trying to interpret a new idea, or formulating the right question for research. This form of literacy, this understanding of scientific method, did not develop overnight. I have spent countless hours each year studying, or even just trying to grasp the subject at hand. It obviously takes patience, determination, and an unceasing source of wonder to keep doing what I do. What some people might not know is that I, along with my peers, have had several specific moments that helped shape who I am today. I did not realize, until I took a recent English class, how much the events in my childhood laid the foundation for what I study today in college.

Throughout my life I have been able to appreciate the hidden messages behind cartoons like the ones found in most newspapers today. They contain simple dialog and artistic and comedic timing to portray a greater message while entertaining the reader. I still flip through textbooks looking for the small cartoons which had little to do with the subject at hand. This love for comics has deep roots in my childhood. My uncle introduced me to *Calvin and Hobbes* when I was nine, maybe ten years old, and I have been hooked ever since. The cartoon is about a little boy and his imaginary tiger who face life's problems and mysteries. As a young boy myself, I quickly became attached to Calvin's harassment of Suzy, his smart and cute next-door neighbor, by throwing snowballs and any gross object he could find. I would stay up past my bedtime and read the strips over and over under the covers with my flashlight. Little did I know at the time that I was beginning to ponder the same deep philosophical questions that Calvin was. I believe this kind of questioning I learned as a kid helped shaped me into becoming a biologist.

One might ask, "How did reading *Calving and Hobbes* shape you into becoming a biologist?" Of course, it was not the sole vehicle in my becoming who I am today; as with most things, there were several other factors. What staying up late reading that cartoon did was get me thinking. More importantly, it caused me to think critically, to analyze what I am examining, to break it apart, to dissect the question, to look at it from different angles. This process is very necessary for a biologist to do and is something that has to be learned. For my major, being able to ask the right questions is an expression of literacy.

Calvin would be wandering through his backyard, which happened to be an elaborate forest with wandering streams, cliffs, and abundant wildlife, and then would come across a piece of trash and go into a speech about man's view on nature. Another time, Calvin might be staring at the stars in awe of how big the universe is and wonder why we make such a big fuss over little things. Calvin could always ask the right questions.

Of course, *Calvin and Hobbes* was not my only childhood memory that had an impact on who I am today. Another source was my introduction to the computer. In middle school, my family purchased our first computer, and at the time it was a big deal for me. Games like *SimCity* and *Age of Empires* instantly captured my imagination. No longer was I pretending to lead militaries with little plastic army men; I was a king controlling my civilization through time: finding and exploiting resources for my economy, trading with neighboring colonies for goods, coming up with diplomatic treaties, and even breaking them and going to war. *Age of Empires* was a very complex game, one that required a lot from a young boy. First, I had to know the lingo, which at times was a completely different language. I also had to know how to solve problems: if my civilization needed gold to upgrade its cavalry into paladins, I was the man who had to make it happen. Without my control, my workers would stand around and scratch their butts; it's not their fault they were never properly educated. I decided their fate, I decided what happened, and I could explore the possibilities of experimentation and watch it happen. This helped develop the problem-solving skills I use constantly today, as well as paving the way to computer literacy.

America Online (AOL), a dialup Internet-access program that has several other features built into it that seemed to be made specifically for kids my age, showed up in my house about the time I was entering seventh grade. My favorite features were the buddy list and instant messaging. The buddy list showed me who was online and who was not. From this window, I could start writing to my friends, and then they could see instantly that I was online, as it popped up on their screens. It was not uncommon for me to be talking to three different people at once for long periods of time. This form of communication, instant messaging, greatly helped my social development and is probably the only reason I can type fluently today. It was not all typing though: AOL showed me the ropes of the computer outside the computer game. It caused me to troubleshoot problems, download and install software, and even understand how a computer works in general. I use these computer skills just as much today as I did ten years ago. In fact, a couple of weeks ago I was trying to use some graphing software, and my computer did not recognize the file type. I knew exactly what it meant and was able to fix the problem. Someone who had yet to receive computer experience might not have been able to understand that. Of course, if I were trying to explain the necessity of computer experience to my parents when I was in middle school, they would have merely laughed.

My parents had a helping hand in my obsession with nature; in fact, some people might say they forced it. Any time I was not doing anything they found productive, I was made to go play outside. At first, it always upset me, because like most kids my age I was rebellious and did not want to do what my parents told me to do. However, it was while I was outside that I first started watching ants carry off sprinkled sugar or birds making nests in trees. It was while I was outside that I released fish into a local pond, and it was while I was outside that I began to love the outdoors. When I started college, I used that love to fuel my desire to understand. Where else is there a better field of study for that purpose than biology?

As I finish up my senior year in college, I cannot help but think of all the things that molded me into who I am today. If Calvin had played inside instead of exploring his world, would I have the ability to question the things I do today? I would like to think I would, but I doubt it. I seriously doubt my interest in the ever-increasing problem of stream eutrophication would have surfaced if I never learned how to ask the right questions. Even if it had, the problem requires me to think in a logical order and to understand cause and effect. Did playing *Age of Empires* really help me do that? I think so. I think the computer helped me better formulate the tables, graphs, and reports I use on a daily basis for my studies in biology. This major requires that special form of literacy one can never learn by reading a textbook. It requires the kind of literacy I have just described. I now realize it was this special form of literacy and the love I developed for nature that steered me toward becoming a biologist.

Sojourn Home: Knocked Up, Not Knocked Out

Lerner Kolb

This essay was written as a memoir for Writing I.

STANDING IN JIM'S BATHROOM in Toledo, the cold, hard, salmon/terracotta Spanish ceramic tiles were pressing up on my bare feet as the two pink lines of a similar color appeared on the pregnancy test instead of one. I thought to myself, "Okay. Okay. Okay. Okay. Okay. Everything is going to be OKAY." I took a couple of deep breaths in through my nose and out through my mouth, and I reached for the cold brass doorknob. It felt like a hundred pounds of resistance turning in my hand before it gave way and pulled in toward me so I could start walking down the stairs toward the living room where Jim was waiting for the results.

He looked like something close to a train wreck when he saw the stick; he seemed like he had been run over by a semi-truck and stayed that way for about three days. I could smell the red sauce bubbling on the stove for dinner, and the weight of it in my nose turned my stomach. In reality, we barely knew each other. I had only been in Toledo for about eight months; I had moved there for business. I operated half a dozen clubs, all of which were cycled out so that we never owned any of them for more than a year or two—except for Titanium in Toledo: that was our cash cow. My job was to move around every six months or so and scout new property. I would then buy the location, gut the inside, supervise the build out, finish the licensing, hire the staff, train the permanent management, and pass it on to them once things were running smoothly; my specialty was the bar and wait staff. We would flip 'em once they profited a million a year. That's real-estate jargon for "buy them cheap, fix them up, and sell them at a profit." Frank was my partner, and he provided the money and the business experience; I did the leg work and made sure everything happened the way it was supposed to. Have you ever seen *Roadhouse*? I was kind of like Patrick Swayze.

We had taken on a two-fer project by hanging onto Titanium in Toledo while starting a new place called The Kiss in Detroit. Since the two were only about forty-five minutes apart, it was fairly easy to manage them simultaneously. I was working about 120 hours a week and felt like walking death at any given point in time. The money was insanely good, but the lifestyle had certainly taken its toll on me. I was burned out and exhausted, and I knew I needed a vacation. I told Francis he would have to cover for me for a week while I disappeared and got some sleep. He knew me well enough to know that if he did not take my word for it, I would probably have a nervous breakdown, so I got my week.

The second day of my vacation I was sitting in a sushi bar. It was a couple of degrees cooler than comfortable, just to remind the patrons that the raw fish was properly refrigerated, and the smell of soy sauce brought the taste of it to my tongue. The bar stools were chrome with padded black saucer seats, and the half-back was stick straight so that it was impossible to ever get comfortable. As a result, every one was left sitting upright as if they were in a job interview or their grandmothers were watching very closely. I noticed the music playing in the background sounded like something from an officer's club in the old Vietnam War movies when this bubbly, blonde-haired, blue-eyed girl named Julie introduced herself and her friends to me. We all started talking as her boyfriend Shawn walked in. Long story short: Shawn and Jim were best friends, and after I knew all of Shawn's obscure records, he introduced us.

I spent the rest of my vacation being wined and dined by the older, charming, handsome mystery that was sitting across the living room from me that night with the pregnancy test in his hand. We went out on Lake Erie on his speedboat and his houseboat, and we drove to Ann Arbor on his motorcycle and went camping. We felt like we had known each other forever and stayed up until dawn talking about everything that came to mind, instead of making ourselves go to sleep.

The novelty faded shortly after nature proved once again that the biological evolution of a species will always take precedence over two people trying to get their rocks off; eventually reproduction always wins. My lifestyle in general did not really scream, "Mommy!" So I gave Frank the sudden, and not so great, news. It was not much longer than a week or two after finding out that I was pregnant that I packed all of my belongings that really mattered into my brand-new, champagne-colored Toyota Corolla and tied my queen-sized pillow-top mattress to the roof of my car with blue nylon ratchet straps for the eleven hour drive home.

I stopped at a Subway for a bite to eat on the Ohio/Illinois border—the sky looked like bedlam was near, and that was the last time during my trip that I saw the sun. I drove straight into a rainstorm, or perhaps it followed right behind me, but either way I was soaked in torrential rain virtually the entire way. By the time I reached Springfield, the plastic wrap that was "protecting" my mattress had completely peeled back from the front and had blown back so that one half of my mattress was a soggy sponge. Everywhere I stopped for gas someone tried to help me rewrap it, but I always graciously declined. It seemed pretty futile at that point and besides, it would dry out eventually. I was just grateful for the dose of rural hospitality. Toledo and Detroit would sooner shoot you than help you—I'll take a good ol' boy in a pickup truck any day.

I will spare you the overly involved, "Then I got fat and pregnant and went through a gruesome delivery" story. Just fast forward to February 6th, 2004; it was the day after Makaio (his name rhymes with Ohio and means, "Gift from God," in Hawaiian) was born, and we were being released from the hospital. All I could think as I loaded him into the car was, "Okay, so I'm really taking this tiny, helpless, complex being home with me now. I have no qualifications for this, everyone's sure they don't want to stop me, right?" There it was, the resounding silence where no one protested and everyone held the peace. I was a parent. This hairy little boiled chicken was my sole responsibility whether he liked it or not. The sentiment was echoed as we walked into the apartment, and I set his carrier down on the floor. He looked up at me for a second, and I felt the hanging pressure of an awkward silence, so I did what any reasonable person would do—I filled it with pointless conversation.

"So, this is home, for now anyway. At some point in the near future, I plan to get a yard for you to run around in. So, just hang tight. Of course, by, 'near future,' I mean in relation to all of eternity, so don't hold your breath either. That crappy, respectable, hourly job I took doesn't really have, 'Lap of Luxury,' written all over it, but we'll get there." By the time the evening was over, Makaio had heard about my political orientation, my spiritual beliefs, and my general moral stance in the world. He seemed to agree, as indicated by the occasional gurgle or coo, but I could tell he was strongly opposed to Hillary in '08 when he let out the biggest dirty diaper you have ever seen just at the mere mention of it.

After a year of infant care, breast feeding, diaper changes, no sleep, and some of the sweetest moments of my life, I decided that our schedule had settled to a point that I might be able to go back to school. I walked onto campus feeling like I had a huge sandwich sign, "LOOK AT THE FREAK. SHE'S NOT BEEN IN CLASS IN EIGHT YEARS, AND THERE'S PROBABLY SOME SPIT-UP SOMEWHERE ON HER CLOTHING." It was a rocky start, but I fell back into stride pretty quickly and remembered that I used to be pretty good at this academic thing. Newly equipped with life-skills that made time management, study skills, and motivation a cakewalk, I realized that I not only belonged here—I flourished here.

Now Makaio is two and he amazes me daily with his stubborn, ornery, hysterical, sweet-natured antics. He has taught me more about love, kindness, patience, and responsibility than twenty-two other years of living combined. We have not just survived the last three years, our life is actually pretty damn good. I wake up every morning around 5:30 and am on campus from 8:00 until 11:00. I work from 11:15 until 5:30 P.M., and then I go pick Makaio up from preschool. We go home and I make dinner, which is done just in time for his bath. Afterwards, we play and read some books until 7:30 P.M. so that he can go to bed. I usually study until my brain hurts and then I quilt. Yes, I am an honorary eighty year-old and I quilt (shut up), while listening to music or watching a movie. I have taken up residence on the Dean's List, I supervise a handful of the most incredible women I have ever had the pleasure of working with, and I am more honest, trustworthy, loving, patient, and understanding than I (or anyone else) ever thought I could be. Makaio is the most incredible, stubborn, sensitive, funny little Buddha I have ever known, and I am enriched more every day by sharing in his life.

Thank you, Monster!

—Love, Momma

Chapter Two:
Sourced Academic Writing

The Line that Cripples Society: Educated vs. Uneducated

Matthew Wilson

This essay was written as a textual analysis for Writing I.

MEASURING A PERSON'S EDUCATION has become a general measuring tool for societal class. While basic education is being required up to a certain age, the economical world is now requiring at least a minimum of a high school diploma for most jobs. Yet, if these systems are in place, why is it that there are still so many Americans who are considered to be uneducated? In his essay, "Learning in the Key of Life," Jon Spayde writes, "There is no divide in American life that hurts more than the one between those we consider well educated and those who are poorly or inadequately schooled" (66).

The best point that Spayde makes is found in his opening remarks:

> What does it mean—and more important, what *should* it mean—to be educated? This is a surprisingly tricky two-sided question. Masquerading as simple problem-solving, it raises a whole laundry list of philosophical conundrums: What sort of society do we want? What is the nature of humankind? How do we learn best? And—most challenging of all—what is the Good? Talking about the meaning of education inevitably leads to the question of what a culture considers most important. (64)

Spayde is correct on several accounts by this series of questions. First, asking what it should mean to be educated. It has become in society that this question is answered by diplomas and degrees from respected educational institutions; one of the most respected higher education institutions in society today is Harvard University. Spayde quotes Henry David Thoreau who states, "I am self educated; that is, I attended Harvard College," Spayde adds, "indeed Harvard in the early 19th century excelled mainly in the extent and violence of its food fights" (66). Now, Harvard is one of the nation's most highly respected universities for academics, but has street smart education mixed into its history.

How does one define a person as being well educated? Is being well educated judged by grades through the course of an academic career? Perhaps instead of focusing on academic test scores, more attention should be paid to life experiences. But in our current society, the level of education is only determined by letters printed on a card and are determined by someone who is thought to be well-versed and highly educated on the subject. The fact is that as complex beings our incredibly complex brains differ greatly enough between people that there cannot truly be a standard set to test intelligence. Rather such standardized testing tests nothing more than our academic book smarts. A person whose mind fails to function fully is automatically deemed unintelligent, when they can be fully capable of leading normal and active lives. The only difference between the so-called unintelligent and the intelligent is that they are not considered to have the ability to perform well when being addressed with questions found on standardized tests. Because of similar lines of thought, standardized testing is not the most effective, and the ever evolving world has tried to solve the problem by means of technology. By requiring employees to learn basic computer skills, one has now forced education upon another, instead of encouraging, and inspiring that person to learn on their own ambition.

Conversely, we have those who have been deemed as being less unintelligent. And by the scores of a standardized, timed test perhaps they cannot perform in a manner such as answering text book questions, but skilled labor and most employment skills come from experience and seizing opportunity, not from anything that can be received from a book. Likewise, most "unintelligent" are more commonly incredible geniuses when it comes to the theory of street smarts. In this case, a person has decided to achieve their success through knowledge by living the experiences of the real world. The smartest person may be able to find the answer to long drawn out textbook questions, but the simple fact is that the one with less intelligence, but greater life knowledge, is more likely to succeed on a long term scale than a person whose life is invested in memorizing books.

Now, the best situation between the two is obviously some middle ground. Where a person, has the ability to read and understand reading well, and at the same time has the abilities of common sense, and general knowledge received by day-to-day life. In corporate America, intelligence is a very important factor, but in order to rise through the levels of business one must possess the street smarts with which to swoon the people who make the top level decisions. They must also be able to establish and maintain a positive persona. Furthermore, to be successful in corporate business, it merely helps to be "educated," but through the proper training and the willingness to sacrifice the good of others, one can easily make his or her way through the ranks of corporate America.

The difference between being educated or uneducated cannot be determined by standardized testing or by the job or career path that person chooses. Education is, then, determined by a person's functionality. It is the fine line determined by those that consider themselves "educated" that metaphysically disables society, and it keeps us from living in a harmonious environment. By judging everyone from this line as being either educated or uneducated, we lose focus on whether or not we are in fact educated, and whether or not that education is strictly book education, street education, or a combination of the two. Until the time when we stop judging people based on education and give them the equal opportunity that is stressed in our society that allows them the chance to perform and succeed, we will not make any progress. Instead, we are simply disqualifying a person who is deemed uneducated from being able to succeed in life.

In Splinters with Atwood

Joe Van Nostrand

This essay was written as a textual analysis for Writing I.

"GIVE ME YOUR TIRED, YOUR POOR, you sang, and for awhile you meant it," Margaret Atwood writes in "A Letter to America," where she expresses her doubts about the United States' integrity these days and explains her fears about the future while making references to what she considers the golden age of America (566). Atwood attempts to make the point that our government is corrupt and in need of change. She does a decent job of defending her point by bringing up examples of modern-day politics and military endeavors as well as concerns for the future, the economy, and America's image to the rest of the world. However, she dwells too much in the past to support her thesis; Atwood does not take into account that times change and no country can be the same forever. She spends too much time in the piece talking about her favorite memories of entertainment from childhood and not enough defending her point.

Atwood writes, "You were the Mickey Mouse and Donald Duck comic books I read," as she refers to popular pastimes she had as a child (565). Many different figures from the past come to life in her piece, though all those she mentions are in the entertainment industry: books, music, and film. None have anything to do with politics or the military unlike the scenarios she mentions later on while talking about the modern-day United States or the future. Atwood writes that "[t]his is a difficult letter to write, because I'm no longer sure who you are," as she leads into her discussion on the media figures she grew up with that were from the U.S. (565). But how does she know the U.S.? She knows it only through entertainment. She makes no mention of any other cultural aspects of the U.S., though she claims to have once known the U.S. She was a child at the time and so she makes mention of a child's things; she didn't pay attention to politics then, or she didn't care, so of course she didn't know the U.S. anymore than many children do today who do not pay attention to current events. Yet she attempts to make an argument in spite of these facts.

As Atwood closes her essay, she writes, "You, too, have great spirits of the past you may call upon: men and women of courage, of conscience, of prescience" (567). Who exactly is she talking about here? Mickey Mouse and Ella Fitzgerald? She makes no mention of anyone in U.S. history in the piece that matches the description of the great spirits of the past. Atwood clarifies, attempting to explain the importance and influence of past figures, "The British used to have a myth about King Arthur. He wasn't dead, but sleeping in a cave, it was said; in the country's hour of greatest peril, he would return" (567). I say "attempting to explain" only because she just states the legend and then goes into the quote that opens this paragraph. This great leader is the only one she mentions in the entire letter, and he isn't even from the United States. A few examples of people who showed courage and intelligence she could have used instead of people like Elvis: Abraham Lincoln, a great President and public speaker who had the mindset to abolish slavery in the U.S.; George Washington, who had the courage to stand up and fight against Britain to gain the colonies their independence at the risk of not only his own life, but all of his friends as well; Franklin Delano Roosevelt, who wasn't afraid to stand up to the Supreme Court to get the programs running needed to get the U.S. out of the Great Depression; even someone such as Dolly Madison, a noble First Lady who, during the War of 1812 and the invasion of Washington D.C., rescued many important state papers and an original portrait of George Washington from the burning White House. And those are just a few. There are countless people she could have mentioned in her paper but chose not to. Why would she choose to do this? Perhaps the reason lies in how much she really pays attention to the news or how much she really cares about our history and the issues we face.

Since she only made mention of issues in the United States that are news-worthy globally, I suspect that she didn't really do any research in writing this piece: war in Iraq, level of debt, the American economy, and rights of citizens being compromised. She makes no mention of other issues we face as a people and only concentrates on the issues that pertain to the Canadian people. For instance, Atwood states, "We know perfectly well that if you go down the plug-hole, we're going with you" (567). While I can see where she has the right to be concerned with where America is heading, why choose to mention American rights being compromised? I suspect to get the reader's attention and alert them to what is going on or maybe Atwood is ensuring that the reader is on her side when she uses emotional appeal by crying "You're gutting the Constitution," "You're running up a record level of debt," and "You're torching the American economy" (567).

Another flawed example of Atwood's is her comparison between the U.S. and the U.S.S.R. Atwood argues that America may begin to be like the U.S.S.R. in that we'll have "lots of tanks, but no air conditioning. That will make folks cross . . . when they can't take a shower because your short-sighted bulldozing of environmental protections has dirtied most of the water and dried up the rest. Then things will get hot and dirty indeed" (567). What is her point here? Atwood seems to be suggesting that we're short sighted and not concerned about the environment at all, but why? Further, why bring this argument into the paper five sevenths of the way through it? This point just popped out of nowhere and is taken nowhere since she then goes on to discuss the American economy.

My overall impression of Margaret Atwood is that she really doesn't know what she's talking about and that she just sat down and started writing with no clear idea as to where she was going with the letter. Atwood seems to do a little bit of rambling about her favorite things as a child. She also fails to mention any great figure of America's past that we can call upon now "to stand with you, to inspire you, to defend the best in you" (567). She appears to not have done a terrible amount of research in relation to the issues in the United States and chose only to attack the issues that are global, and not the ones we deal with in our own borders. Atwood also appears to do a lot of assuming: that we'll end up like the U.S.S.R., that the U.S. may one day end up looking like a joke to the other countries of the world. Atwood does not do a good job of defending her choice at all, and the next time she chooses to write this type of paper, she should try knowing what the heck she's talking about first.

Works Cited

Atwood, Margaret. "A Letter to America." *The Presence of Others: Voices and Images That Call for Response.* 4th ed. Eds. Andrea A. Lunsford and John J. Ruszkiewicz. Boston: Bedford/St. Martin's, 2004. 565–567.

From the Rack to the Classroom

Howard Simmons

This essay was written for Writing II: Academic Writing.

THE FIRST COMIC BOOK I REMEMBER reading (at least in any detail) was a three-part series entitled *The Many Deaths of Batman*. I was in the fourth grade of elementary school and Tim Burton's film *Batman* had recently been released—much to the delight of ten year-old boys everywhere. The movie and its brooding hero sent me giddily to the nearest comic book rack, which was haphazardly placed at the back of the magazine aisle of my hometown's grocery store.

Throughout most of junior high school years and on into the first year of high school, I read happily and greedily page upon page of panels: some stories told gaudily and brightly colored, others black and white and heavy with atmosphere.

As I entered high school and began to consider myself an adult, I came to see comics as something childish and a source of embarrassment. A staple of science fiction geeks, comics would only hinder my pursuit of acceptance among my peers and impede my growth into maturity. And, like others who relegate childhood pleasures to the stable of memories in order to pursue adulthood, I eventually placed all my comics in a box and pushed them to the back of the closet. Novels became my means of escape and recreation.

It wasn't until I had safely entered my twenties that I rediscovered my love for comics and realized they could offer more than mesmerizing stories of vengeance-seeking men clad in spandex. I had picked up a copy of artist Daniel Clowes's *David Boring*, a murder mystery set on an island after the world may have come to an end.

As comic books have developed, beginning with their creation and booming popularity during World War II to the current myriad graphic novels in circulation today, they have steadily, but not without a fight, begun to build a reputation as more than childish recreation. Works such as Art Spiegelman's *Maus*, Will Eisner's *A Contract with God* (which Eisner himself proclaimed as the first graphic novel), and Alan Moore's *The Watchmen* have pushed the reader's knowledge of what a comic can be. Their topics range from superheroes to memoirs. They can be written for children—*Casper the Friendly Ghost*—or strictly for adults: Frank Miller's graphically violent and sexual *Sin City*.

The acceptance of comics and graphic novels—which consist of lengthier pieces of work or a collection of smaller vignettes that form a cohesive narrative when grouped together in panel-by-panel overlay—as a valid form of creative expression and high art has been more readily granted in the art community. Renee French, an artist whose work is featured primarily in comic format, has received praise as well as the chance to exhibit her artwork in museums such as the Swiss Institute in New York City. The embracement of the art community is more forthcoming to different forms of expression, while it is harder to gain in the literary community, often viewed as stodgy and elitist.

As graphic novels have gained in popularity and acceptance, the literary and education communities have come to see some worth in the form, primarily as a tool for education and an introduction to other, so-called *higher* literary devices. Rich Shea, writing for *Teacher Magazine*, points out that many educators nationwide are using comic books as literacy tools. Graphic novels and comic books have proven an effective way to capture the attention of students who may be less than interested in reading. However, the use of graphic novels as a "stepping stone" also implies that it is still a less respected form. The graphic novel continues to waver on unsteady literary ground.

There is some debate about the artistic medium under which comic books should be classed. Undoubtedly, it is a primarily visual form, structured much like a film: readers move from one panel to the next, their eyes focusing first on the art then drifting to the written words comprising the character's dialogue, inner thoughts, or separate narrative voice. The minimal space given to the written word often demands conciseness of language and a skillful command of conveying briefly all that the writer intends or needs to say. When written effectively, language can heighten, sustain, or illuminate subtle emotions or offer a narrative structure to guide the artist in what he or she is trying to convey.

Some might argue that the very fact that so much importance is placed on the visual aspect of the graphic novel can't support the theory that it is also literature. But I would argue that the very complexity denotes a new form of literature, one in which the marriage of visuals and linguistics add another piece to the artistic puzzle, further conveying the uniqueness of human existence. As time progresses, so do the ways in which generations express themselves.

Peter Schjeldahl writes for *The New Yorker* that "graphic novels—pumped-up comics—are to many in their teens and twenties what poetry once was, before bare words lost their cachet." A recent advertisement for a local art show in the Springfield, Missouri, area claimed that words were no longer the medium in which ideas were conveyed. As the world becomes increasingly streamlined, the visual medium becomes the fastest way to receive information. The artist/author of the graphic novel, when at the height of talent, can often convey the complexity of human emotions with a single panel and a few carefully written words.

In the 1980s, comic book writer Alan Moore showed the world that comics, specifically the superhero genre, could offer a plethora of ideas. The story of *The Watchmen*, set in an alternate 1980s where the Cold War still rages, focuses on a group of retired crime fighters who are being murdered by a masked serial killer. Moore switches effectively between pages of written word and the comic format, able to link and thereby show the differences and similarities between two supposedly separate identities. The result is a gripping, surprisingly emotional story that focuses on the regrets, failures, and mundane lives of those who had given of themselves for a larger ideal. Moore has consistently defied expectations and refuses to allow himself to be marginalized. A smarter, less sensational provocateur than fellow artist Frank Miller, his works increase dialogue about the medium, further the exchange of ideas, and, above all, use the medium in a way which tells a story to the best of his ability.

With the theatrical release of Frank Miller's *Sin City* in 2004, the cult graphic novels of the same name suddenly received a glaring spotlight of attention from the media. Mimicking Miller's stark black and white pages punctured by splashes of bawdy colors, the movie was an unrelenting phantasmagoria of violence, hyper-sexuality, and gore. It was a raging success. *Sin City's* neo-noir stories illustrate perfectly the progression of a medium that was primarily seen as something for children and now places it firmly in adult territory. Its stories of prostitution, cannibalism, and mass murder are anything but child's fare.

Not all graphic novels are as sensational, however. Comic artists and writers such as Daniel Clowes, author of *Ghost World* and *Ice Haven*, and Chris Ware, author of *Jimmy Corrigan: The Smartest Boy in the World*, have garnered respect in both the art and literary community. *Ghost World*, the story of two girls who are in flux between high school and adulthood, is a strange, heart-wrenching account of displacement to which most of its readers can relate. Clowes's work "plays crisp, bland cartooning, at times reminiscent of the old *Can You Draw This?* matchbook ads, against stealthily nuanced writing" (Schjeldahl, *New Yorker*). It is only because of Clowes' talent as a writer that Schjeldahl uses the term "stealthily nuanced." Clowes' ability as a writer helps the artwork take on an additional dimension and offers new wonders to the reader.

In 1992, Art Spiegelman won the Pulitzer Prize for his story, *Maus: A Survivor's Tale*. Drawing Jews as mice and Germans as cats, Spiegelman told the story of his father's internment in a concentration camp. His use of anthropomorphism allowed him to tell a terrible, horrifying story in a way that subdued the more exploitative elements and heightened the horror and emotional impact for the reader.

Because of the varying genres of graphic novels, their importance as artistic expression can often be overlooked. The graphic novel's relegation in scholars' minds as an effective tool for education, while valid, marginalizes its impact. There are critics who argue that most comics used in classrooms are either dumbed-down or too inappropriate (Shea 16). This is not an entirely fair assessment, since it has been stated that graphic novels require more cognitive skills (Schwarz 262). As Schjeldahl writes, "Consuming them—toggling for hours between the incommensurable functions of reading and looking—is taxing" (162). Schejeldahl even states that reading comics demands and rewards mental flexibility and nervous stamina. He further supposes in his article that graphic novels have come of age. His view, while held by others, denotes a conception of the graphic novel and comic books in general as a passing movement, although others would argue that it is still progressing as a medium.

One could argue that as literature changes and adapts, so too will the graphic novel. The graphic novel should be viewed neither as a lesser literary genre nor as a mere tool to catch the interest of illiterate children, but rather as a different form of art—a marriage of artistic and literary capabilities. The graphic novel still offers a plethora of new ideas and visions that readers have yet to discover.

Works Cited

Clowes, Daniel. "Blue Italian Shit." *Caricature*. Seattle: Fantagraphic Books. 25–31.

- - -. *David Boring.* New York: Pantheon Books, 2000.

- - -. *Ghost World.* Seattle: Fantagraphic Books, 1998.

Eisner, Will. *A Contract With God.* New York: DC Comics.

Moore, Alan. *Watchmen.* New York: DC Comics, 1995.

Nadel, Dan. "The Dark Stuff." Print Mar/Apr 2006: 70–75.

Schwarz, Gretchen E. "Graphic Novels for Multiple Literacies." *Journal of Adolescent and Adult Literacy* Nov. 2002: 262–65.

Schjeldahl, Peter. "Words and Picture: Graphic Novels Come of Age." *The New Yorker* 81 (2005): 162–68.

Second Baptist Church. Advertisement. *KY3*. Sept. 2006

Shea, Rich. "Comics in the Classroom." *Teacher Magazine* Oct. 2006: 16–17.

Spiegelman, Art. *Maus: A Survivor's Tale.* New York: Pantheon.

Chocolate is a Girl's Best Friend

Melissa Scott

This essay was written for Writing I.

BEFORE THE TIME OF CORTEZ and Columbus, Aztec natives were making chocolate. It was a food so highly desired that it was only served to "nobles, priests, and warriors"; Aztec woman, unfortunately, were not allowed to partake in eating this "food of the gods" (Cooper). Throughout the rest of history, chocolate traveled all over the world as a delicacy. Finally, it made its way back to North America when the colonists came over from Europe. Since then, chocolate has spread to the homes of Americans and the shelves of convenience stores everywhere. According to Sandra Yin, "In 2000, total U.S. chocolate consumption rose to 3.3 billion pounds. . . . That's almost 12 pounds for every man, woman and child in the U.S." But even this sweet delight has found a place in the gender code. Though chocolate is consumed by men and women alike, American culture views chocolate as a feminine product as a result of persuasive advertising and women's natural attraction to chocolate.

Men are often seen giving women flowers and chocolates on dates. Valentine's Day chocolates are sold all over in frilly hearts that express affection. Chocolate is often given feminine-like descriptions, such as "smooth," "sweet," and "soft." It is obvious that chocolate has been labeled as "the one thing a woman craves." I mean, have you ever heard a guy say, "Wow, I just really need some chocolate right now." If you have, you may be one of few.

Women do crave chocolate at certain times. It is estimated that "40% of woman crave chocolate before and after their menstrual period" which may be explained by the theory that chocolate boosts "deficiencies in the body" during the monthly cycle ("Chocolate and Women"). These cravings usually begin at the age when girls start maturing into women. And when a moody teenager is PMSing, what better way to chill her out than with a piece of chocolate—or two, or three? The chemicals in chocolate may make women feel better. The sugar, on one hand, is said to release serotonin, which "reduces depression or anxious feelings"; on the other hand, chocolate contains many other substances that are believed to provide a "mental boost, stimulate the nervous system and heart rate, and produce feelings of euphoria" ("Chocolate . . ."). Chocolate may also cause a psychological effect: since American women tend to count calories and watch their fat intake, chocolate is seen as an "indulgence" ("Chocolate . . .). Of course, with all the stuff a woman is expected to do nowadays such as drive kids around, work in a fast-paced business, do housework, feed the family, and in general make sure life is going smoothly, a woman could use a little indulgence now and again. Such biological and psychological functions of chocolate would obviously increase most women's want of the brown, sugary substance.

As we girls begin to grow and mature, we are introduced to chocolate not in any medical way, but in a cultural way. Our mothers, who were let in on these "womanly" secrets when they hit their teen years, pass it on almost as a rite of passage. As soon as our first menstrual cycle starts, they are right there with a chocolate bar in their hands. They tell us it gets you through the stress and anxiety of being a woman. It's the one thing that can make a bad day a little less depressing. It also helps to calm one's self down as the roller coaster of mood swings start to buzz in our brains. Almost any girl will tell you that they and their mothers have a connection with chocolate. And then that connection spreads out to other female friends and relatives, making it a social, cultural experience that many women can feel a part of. Chocolate is that brown, creamy stuff that holds us together.

To an advertising company, this information is pure gold. Since Americans already have labeled chocolate as a more feminine food, the advertising companies have not only run with the idea, they are increasing its spread. In his essay, "Men's Men and Women's Women," Steve Craig explains, "Gender commercials, like gendered programs, are designed to give pleasure to the target audience, since it is the association of the product with a pleasurable experience that forms the basis for much American television advertising" (163). Since women get the most pleasure out of chocolate, they are therefore the target of chocolate companies. Rita Clifton points out, "'Women are the key to chocolate advertising" (qtd. in Cooper).

But chocolate manufacturers didn't stop with just targeting pleasure:

they took their advertising to a whole new level. During WWII, manufacturers urged that chocolates should be bought for "female air raid wardens" to provide them with enough energy and nutrition (Cooper). This angle was used to reach the working women of America during the war, and as women's roles changed with the times, so did the chocolate advertisements (Cooper). With your housewives, you had your practical chocolate. With the hippie women of the 1960s, you had your freewill chocolate. Eventually, chocolate advertisements took the form of chocolate being seen as a little dangerous—it was given sex appeal. Then you had your low-fat chocolate for the healthy girl when obesity became a problem for many women.

Today we see hard working women on television basking in a moment of peace and quiet with their favorite candy bar. Advertisers have taken on the relaxed, sophisticated type of marketing, pushing high quality chocolates to indulge the senses of the classy woman (Cooper). Now, if you sit down and watch the commercials in between television shows, you will see a beautiful woman on the screen away from all distractions, eating chocolate so slowly you wonder if she'll ever finish it. It gives women the sense that they too can be sexy, stylish, and relaxed. With our fast paced society, these commercials are highly attractive. And by targeting women with these publicity tactics, companies are also reaching the rest of their family members. Since most women do the shopping in the family, which is also seen as a feminine activity, they buy chocolate not only for themselves but for their kids. And kids love candy. So do men.

It is now the fashion to rebel against gender code standards and expectations, and it is surprising that not many people have even uttered a word about how chocolate is not just a feminine product. Maybe people just don't realize it until they are actually confronted with the thought that we do indeed tend to lean the concept of chocolate more to the feminine side. Or maybe people just don't care. Or perhaps it's that we like to categorize chocolate as feminine, accept it in our subconscious as such, and feel completely comfortable with the idea. Many women would probably tell you that they like to think of chocolate as feminine because it makes them feel better about themselves, and it's a little piece of culture that woman can relate to. Even though many people eat chocolate no matter what their gender, America has placed it in the women's world, and Americans tend to like it just where it is. Especially women.

Note: This essay was completed under the influence of chocolate for inspiration, for taste, and for getting me through stressful writing blocks. Thank you, Aztecs.

Works Cited

"Chocolate and Women." *Sound Medicine*. 14 Feb. 2004. *Indiana University School of Medicine*. 3 Feb. 2007 <http://soundmedicine.iu.edu/segment.php4?seg=71>.

Cooper, Glenda. "Women and Chocolate: Simply Made for Each Other." *Chocolate*. 13 Mar. 2004. *The Times*. 3 Feb. 2007 <http://www.chocolate.org/choclove/women.html>.

Craig, Steve. "Men's Men and Women's Women." *Signs of Life in the USA: Readings on Popular Culture for Writers*. Eds. Sonia Maasik and Jack Solomon. Boston: Bedford/St. Martin's, 2006.

Yin, Sandra. "Constant Cravings—Chocolate Consumption in the US, 2000—Brief Article—Statistical Data Included." *Find Articles*. 1 May 2002. *American Demographics*. 4 Feb. 2007 <http://www.findarticles.com/p/articles/mi_m4021/ is_2002_May_1/ ai_ 88679456>.

Organic Foods: Should We Abandon or Embrace Them?

Julie Whitson

> This essay was written for Writing II: Academic Writing. It uses APA style and is one way to write an annotated bibliography with some conclusions added.

Introduction

RECENTLY, PEOPLE HAVE THROWN the debate about organic foods into the limelight. Some supporters say that organic food drastically reduces environmental problems, supports a good cause, and that the difference in taste and nutrients seems obvious. Opponents claim that the entire organic movement poses a threat to productivity and efficiency in the agricultural market. So the question remains: Should we go with what we know and currently do, or should we aim to support a grassroots movement that could deliver us from environmental consequences? Organic food may not possess every positive quality that its supporters say it does, but the organic foods movement supports good-natured goals, such as limiting farm workers' exposure to harmful pesticides, reducing environmental consequences, and lessening animal exposure to pesticides and antibiotics.

Review 1

IN THE ARTICLE "REDISCOVERING the Human Biosphere" published in *Consumer Health Newsletter*, David Suzuki (2005) describes his opinions about the organic movement from the perspective of a genetic scientist. He asserts that even if we cannot foresee the potential problems that new technology will present years down the road, we should at least understand that the water we drink, the air we breathe, and the land on which we live and grow our food will always play a vital role in our survival. In the 1930s, scientists unleashed a chemical named Dichloro-Diphenyl-Trichloroethane (DDT) that targeted pesky bugs like mosquitoes. Even though the scientific community had conducted many experiments on how well it could perform, the article reminds readers of Rachel Carson's book *Silent Spring*, which presented evidence that DDT affected organisms other than insects, like fish, birds, and ultimately human beings (p. 2).

When technology led to the discovery of chlorofluorocarbons (CFCs) to use as filler in aerosol cans, Suzuki (2005) explains how a similar situation ensued. CFCs did not react with active ingredients in the cans they filled; however, once consumers deposited them into the air, they floated into the upper portion of our atmosphere and their interaction with ultra-violet rays produced free-floating atoms that literally ate away at the ozone layer. Only until several million pounds of CFCs had accumulated did we realize a problem existed.

Review 2
DDT AND CFCS DO NOT POSE the only problems to our environment. Tina Adler (2002) indicates in the article "Harmful Farming," published in *Environmental Health Perspectives*, that agricultural practices today not only add pollutants and other harmful items to our environment, but they also shut down local farm economies and waste natural resources, like fossil fuels, topsoil, and water. The agriculture industry's widespread use of pesticides since the 1950s leaves some people skeptical as to whether or not the sheer volume of pesticides farmers use to get the job done today truly helps the growing of crops. According to Adler (2002), "Crops absorb only one-third to one-half of fertilizer applications, and less than one percent of applied pesticide reaches the target pests" (p. 256). Runoff carries the unused pesticides to area waterways, accounting for 70% of the river and stream pollution in the United States.

As decades ago with DDT and other pesticides currently used, Adler (2002) states that as of 1990, pesticides have caused 500 species to become immune to the strains of pesticides that are used today (p. 256). Unfortunately for the agriculture industry, it is not only pesticide overuse that creates problems; according to Adler (2002), "Seventy percent of antibiotics produced in the United States are fed to healthy animals as growth promoters" (256). The staggering amount of antibiotics fed to animals to prevent infection contributes to the worldwide problem of antibiotic resistance. In the same fashion that bugs mutate to overcome the latest poisons meant to kill them, bacteria worldwide have started to mutate to get around the effects that antibiotics used to have on them. By overexposing bacteria to antibiotics, we give bacteria more opportunities to mutate into something that can resist our current antibiotics.

Review 3

THE OVERALL DIFFERENCE IN TASTE and nutrients in organic food is not always evident, but Marion Nestle (2005) agrees with Adler (2002) in the article "In Praise of the Organic Environment" published in *Global Agenda* that the difference between organic foods and regularly grown foods may not seem overwhelming, but one can find the difference in what organic foods do for the environment. Since 1990, sales each year have gone up by about 20 percent, and in 2004 organic foods pulled in roughly 20 billion dollars (p. 218). This tells us that in some way organic foods have succeeded in making their mark. People who oppose organic foods say that no difference exists between organic and regular foods except the price; however, Nestle (2005) reveals just what it takes for foods to earn an organic certification:

> [The producers] did not use any synthetic pesticides, herbicides, or fertilizers to grow crops or feed for animals; they did not use crops of feed that had been genetically modified, fertilized with sewage sludge or irradiated; they did not feed animals the by-products of other animals; . . . and they were inspected to make sure they followed the rules in letter . . . (p. 218).

When comparing organic and regular foods, one will notice the difference in price first and foremost. Obtaining USDA organic certification in the United States is still not easy. The fee for certification remains costly, most organic farms maintain a higher and fairer working wage, organic farms operate on a smaller scale in order to tend to agriculture as they see fit, and organic farms do not receive government subsidies like other farmers in the agriculture industry. Some opponents of organic foods question the productivity factor on an organic farm; however, research conducted over a period of years shows that "farmers who converted from conventional to organic methods experienced small declines in yields, but these losses were offset by lower fuel costs and better conserved soils" (Nestle, 2005, p. 219). Both of these benefits to organic farmers show direct benefits to the environment.

Many critics also question the safety of some organic methods, such as using manure. Even the manure must meet a certification standard to ensure that the food gets the necessary nutrients *without* the harmful microbes (2% fecal contaminants on traditionally grown, 4% on certified organic, and 11% on produce said to be organic, but not certified) (Nestle, 2005, p. 219). In short, organic foods' "true value comes from what they do for farm workers in lower pesticide exposure, for soils in enrichment and conservation, for water supplies in less fertilizer runoff . . . for fish in protection against contamination with organic hydrocarbons, and for other such environmental factors" (Nestle, 2005, p. 219).

Discussion

THE ORGANIC MOVEMENT PROVIDES a solution to the problems we face dealing with pesticides and the environment. Suzuki (2005) reminds us that we have obviously had problems in the past with chemicals like DDT and CFCs affecting the environment, but only when people spotted the damage did we do something about it. As Hyla Cass (2006) says in her article titled "Environmental Toxin Imbalances" about a recent British study, "The most alarming finding was that 99 percent of those tested had residues of the pesticide DDT in their blood, despite the fact that it had been banned decades ago" (p. 26). The pesticide worked its way up the food chain and effected many aspects of the environment. Even though the government eventually banned DDT, the original pest insects have still developed biological adaptations to this pesticide just as they do to similar pesticides used today.

The United States currently outdoes all other countries in their pesticide usage according to an article in *Essence*, accounting for half of the worldwide usage—two billion pounds a year (Wiltz, 1994, p.24). However, this sheer amount of pesticide usage does not just come from the large agricultural base in our economy. Applying pesticides as much as we do illustrates the problems we face with bugs becoming resistant to the chemicals we currently overuse.

When arguing for organic foods, some activists raise the supposed notion that organic food tastes better and has more nutrients. Scientists cannot quantify these opinions and only found a slightly elevated level of nutrients in certain organic foods. As a personal health benefit, organic foods do not offer a distinct advantage. However, by supporting the organic food movement, one can also make a statement about environmental factors, such as using pesticides, protecting wildlife from groundwater runoff and contamination, and helping to lessen soil erosion. By buying organic foods, one can also help small, local farms survive and stop farm workers' exposure to harmful pesticides, which have been proven to cause certain types of cancer and endocrine damage in the human body. These chemicals affect anyone, especially children, who come in contact with them before they shower and change clothes. The sheer amount of pesticides the United States currently uses (50% of world expenditure) could also point to our quick fix solution to bugs' biological adaptation to current pesticides.

Conclusion

THE ARGUMENTS SURROUNDING THIS TOPIC seems slanted from both perspectives, but this movement at least supports good-natured goals, such as limiting farm workers' exposure to harmful pesticides, limiting environmental consequences, and lessening animal exposure to pesticides and antibiotics. The organic movement poses a solution to the problems that surround the overuse of pesticides and fertilizers before we reach a point in which we must take drastic measures to repair the damage that we have already done. The environmental problems caused by pesticides have not yet reached a peak in which activism has become necessary to avoid permanent damage. The organic foods movement seems so controversial because no one has proven a direct correlation with irreversible damage and the need to act now. Even if we cannot verify direct personal benefits from organic food, remember that purchasing organic food will make a statement about an issue that concerns all aspects of the environment.

References

Adler, T (2002). Harmful farming. *Environmental Health Perspectives*, 110 (5), p. 256. Retrieved March 14, 2007, from Academic Search Premier database.

Cass, H (2006). Environmental toxin imbalances. *Total Health*, 28 (1), p. 26-30. Retrieved March 11, 2007, from Alt Health Watch database.

Nestle, M (2005). In praise of the organic environment. *Global Agenda*, 3, p. 218-19. Retrieved March 11, 2007, from Academic Search Premier database.

Suzuki, D (2005). Rediscovering the human place in the biosphere. *Consumer Health Newsletter*, 28 (2), p. 2-4. Retrieved March 11, 2007, from Alt Health Watch database.

Wiltz, T (1994). Bugging out. *Essence*, 25 (2), p. 24. Retrieved March 14, 2007, from Academic Search Premier database.

Chapter Three:
Longer Sourced Academic Writing

Social Anxiety Disorder: A Personal Struggle with Social Situations

Leanne Colagio

This essay was written as an I-Search for Writing I.

A FEW YEARS AGO, I heard of social anxiety disorder. I learned that it is basically extreme discomfort or anxiety in social situations. I knew that social anxiety causes a lot of people to avoid situations, but I didn't know all of its symptoms, what causes it, and what treatments are available. I wanted to know more about those things because it sounded like it could be the answer to why I act in certain ways in social situations.

For example, I have always been the type of person who absolutely dreads social situations. I find any excuse possible to avoid having to go where there are big gatherings of people. Most people look forward to parties or big group trips. I am the total opposite; I spend days beforehand trying to think of any possible way to get out of going.

My problems are not just limited to big groups. I do not like to be in a position where a lot of attention will be on me, such as interrupting someone, walking into class late, or raising my hand in class to ask a question. I often avoid meeting gazes with people or act like I don't see them so I don't have talk to them, not because I think I'm too good to be caught talking to them, but because I fear that the other person doesn't want to talk to me.

I realize it is ridiculous logic, and it's not normal, but I really can't break out of these habits. People tell me I should just stop caring what other people think, but even when I try my hardest to ignore those thoughts, I cannot. When I heard about social anxiety disorder, I thought that if this disorder was my problem, I could find ways to overcome it. I could find help. After many years of dealing with social anxiety, I can finally define it and get help to be more comfortable in social situations.

Since I didn't know very much about social anxiety disorder, I wanted to gain more knowledge to better understand whether or not my feelings and problems were because of this disorder. I also hoped that while researching, I could find out who I should talk to in order to get help.

I decided the first thing I should do is find as much information as I could on what social anxiety disorder is. So, I went to the Duane G. Meyer Library, where I found some sources that sounded useful and checked out three books and two pamphlets about the disorder. The books I found were each helpful in different ways. For example, *Shy Children, Phobic Adults* by Deborah C. Beidel and Samuel M. Turner focused not only on the diagnosis and treatment for adults but also for children and adolescents as well. Beidel and Turner state, "Although the average age of onset for social phobia has been considered to be mid-adolescence, several authors . . . reported that children as young as age 8 can be diagnosed with the disorder" (36). Since I have been dealing with my problems for a few years now, it seems like I fit into the age group that this disorder affects.

Throughout my research, I found a lot of information that helped me to better understand the disorder. A pamphlet issued by the National Institute of Mental Health (NIMH), *Facts about Social Phobia*, gave this explanation of what social anxiety is: "Social anxiety is a disorder characterized by overwhelming anxiety and excessive self-consciousness in everyday social situations." It went on to explain, "People with social phobia have a persistent, intense, and chronic fear of being watched and judged by others and being embarrassed or humiliated by their own actions" (*People with Social Phobia*). I found that embarrassment and humiliation seem to be the main fears of the people who suffer from this disorder. Most sufferers will go out of their way to avoid these feelings, which often means they will hold themselves back from success. According to Franklin Schneier and Lawrence Welkowitz, "When the excessive fear and anxiety persist, causing a person to forgo important activities and resulting in significant impairment of social life or work, the result is considered a disorder" (9).

This pamphlet also explored some of the variations of social anxiety disorder: "Social phobia can be limited to only one type of situation— such as a fear of speaking in formal on informal situations . . . or in most severe form, may be so broad that a person experiences symptoms almost anytime they are around other people" (NIMH). While I do get very nervous and anxious before giving presentations and speeches, I think I have a more moderate form since I am almost always worrying about what others are thinking of me.

Another pamphlet provided by the NIMH, *A Real Illness: Social Phobia*, provided a checklist of common problems that people facing social anxiety come up against. This list makes it more clear what someone with social anxiety might think or feel:

- I have an intense fear that I will do or say something and embarrass myself in front of other people.
- I am always very afraid of making a mistake and being watched and judged by other people.
- My fear of embarrassment makes me avoid doing things I want to do or speaking to people.
- I worry for days or weeks before I have to meet new people.
- I blush, sweat a lot, tremble, or feel like I have to throw up before and during an event where I am with new people.
- I usually stay away from social situations such as school events and making speeches.

Even though social anxiety disorder is not commonly heard of, it is very common. According to NIMH's pamphlet *Facts about Social Phobia*, "About 3.7% of the US population ages 18 to 24—approximately 5.3 million Americans—has social phobia in any given year." *Anxiety Disorders* by Michelle G. Craske further reveals that "social phobia is the most common of all the anxiety disorders" (209). If this disorder is as common as these statistics suggest, then there is a good chance that I have it.

I also learned that there were treatments available. Craske provides a section about cognitive-behavioral approaches to social phobia, which include the step-by-step process of Heimberg's Cognitive-Behavioral Group Therapy. According to Craske, the theory "consists of simulated exposures to feared situations in-session, cognitive restructuring, and in vivo exposures between sessions" (223). After reading about this group treatment, I felt that it could be very helpful because it takes things slowly and creates a comfortable place where the members can learn to overcome certain social situations that could normally cause anxiety.

Another source I found was a great resource for people like me who would rather try to work through their problems on their own: *The*

Hidden Faces of Shyness: Understanding and Overcoming Social Anxiety, by Schneier and Welkowitz. It is a self-help book that examines cases of people who have dealt with social anxiety in order to make it easier to understand. Schneier and Welkowitz provide self-tests, a self-help program, and information on professional help and where to find it. According to Schneier and Welkowitz, "Research has proven that people with social phobias can make changes and usually do change—when they use the right techniques" (148). The technique they provide "focuses on *constructing* a new set of coping skills (a positive goal), rather than a negative task of *eliminating* a fear" (Schneier and Welkowitz 149).

After reading through all of my material, I decided I needed to find more information. I went back to the library, but this time I used the computer lab and found some sources through EBSCO about social anxiety. Since I already had plenty of general information about social anxiety, I decided to focus my search on all the possible causes and the current drug treatments. I used EBSCO instead of an Internet search engine because I know that some websites are not as credible as many people believe them to be.

One source I found during my search was "Why Do Some Individuals Develop Social Phobia?: A Review with Emphasis on the Neurobiological Influences" by Maria Tillfors. Tillfors writes, "A number of studies in clinical populations have consistently found higher rates of social phobia in relatives of social phobia probands (approximately a two- to threefold increased risk) in comparison to relatives of control probands" (268). One might conclude that if someone's parent experiences problems with social anxiety, then he or she could too. This problem could either be due to genetics or parental influence. My mother was never one to socialize. In fact, I cannot recall a time when I saw my mother include herself in a group of people that were not members of our family. Maybe my social problems came in part from my mother.

Some psychologists suggest that social anxiety is due to a genetic temperament. According to Tillfors, "Temperament research in the past decade has focused on the temperamental construct behavioral inhibition, which is characterized largely by withdrawal, wariness, avoidance and shyness, as well as heightened physiological arousal in novel situations" (269). Predisposed temperament is a possible explanation of social anxiety disorder since the characteristics of behavioral inhibition match some of the characteristics of social anxiety.

Other explanations which could go hand in hand with predisposition look at the interaction between certain neurotransmitters and the amygdala. The amygdala is the part of the brain that controls anger and fear. David G. Myers, author of *Psychology*, explains, "Fear-learning experiences can traumatize the brain, by creating fear circuits within the amygdala" (655). In social situations, fear-learning experiences such as a negative reaction from someone create fear circuits. However, because there are many different attributions of this disorder, it is hard to locate a single cause.

Luckily, there are many ways to help someone overcome this disorder. Almost all of my sources pointed to a variety of ways to get help. An easy first step could be trying to deal with the problem through self-help. There are also many professional options, such as medications and psychological therapies. Medication options discussed by Beidel and Turner include, "tricyclic antidepressants (TCAs), selective serotonin reuptake inhibitors (SSRIs), monoamine oxidase inhibitors (MAOIs), beta-blockers, high-potency benzodiazepines, and the atypical anxiolytic agent azaspirone" (143). Therapies discussed by Schneier and Welkowitz include cognitive-behavioral, group or individual therapy, traditional psychotherapies, and relaxation therapies (208–212).

Another source I found was "Social Anxiety Disorder: Current Treatment Recommendations" by Jacqueline E. Muller, Liezl Koen, Soraya Seedat, and Dan J. Stein. This source went over the different drug treatments available, such as inhibitors and antidepressants. According to it, "pharmacotherapy and psychotherapy were able to effect a decrease in cerebral blood flow in the amygdala, hippocampus, and surrounding cortical areas (all involved in defense reactions to threat) in patients with SAD," or social anxiety disorder (380). If blood flow was decreased to the areas where defense reactions such as anxiety and fear are created, the areas would slow down and not produce as much anxiety. With a lower amount of anxiety, many of the symptoms of social anxiety could be overcome.

The authors also discussed other aspects of the disorder, such as its co-morbidity. Co-morbidity is when there is more than one disorder present, such as a person with social anxiety disorder also having depression. They contend that "[i]t is particularly important to assess for co-morbid psychiatric disorders, which are present in ≥80% of patients with SAD; the most common of these are depression, other anxiety disorders, and substance use disorders" (379). This statistic shows how important it is to get help for those with this disorder, since other disorders often accompany it. It also shows that it is sometimes helpful to take inhibitors and antidepressants, because they can treat both social anxiety and co-morbid disorders such as depression.

After my search in the library, I decided to find a professional who I could interview in the Counseling and Testing Center. I knew it would be a good place to get an interview, because the Counseling Center is staffed by licensed psychologists and counselors, so they would be knowledgeable about social anxiety. I was able to speak with the director of the center, Doug Greiner.

My interview with Greiner provided the most influential information I received up to this point, but some of it was not in the way I had expected. Greiner was very insightful about the symptoms and treatments for social anxiety. One of the new things I learned from my interview with him is that some people develop social anxiety from bad experiences with social situations. Greiner said that a way to combat this anxiety is to "enter a situation briefly and then leave: having a few good experiences tends to decrease the anxiety."

After he talked to me about social anxiety disorder, he asked how I ended up doing a paper on that subject. I told him that I chose it because I thought I had the disorder, and I wanted to know more about it. He surprised and ultimately disappointed me by saying the same thing that I had heard from everyone else to whom I had expressed my thoughts. He told me that it is very easy for someone to start researching a topic in the medical or psychological field and automatically believe that he or she has the disorder.

I did not know what to think. A licensed professional did not believe me. Although we did not talk personally about my problems—the conversation basically ended there because I did not feel it would be polite or proper to contest what he suggested—I was disheartened by the fact that it seemed no one believed I had a problem. I felt like it was becoming pointless to try to get help since everyone I confided in thought I was exaggerating or being a hypochondriac. I ultimately decided I would instead use this project as a way to find ways I could help myself overcome my problems, whether I had this disorder or not.

The truth is, after researching so much about social anxiety disorder, I began to have doubts about whether I had it. A rather interesting online article came to my attention late in my search. This article raises the question of whether shyness is over-diagnosed as social anxiety disorder. In the article, *The Times* suggest, "Shyness, once an accepted and even admired trait, has been hijacked and given the status of a syndrome. Some experts believe that half the population now 'suffer' from it. But is it natural or a medical affliction?"

If this article is true, maybe I am just a normal shy person. Since my life is not governed by my fears of social situations, I began to doubt that I actually suffered from social anxiety disorder. While I do get uncomfortable in some social situations and try to avoid them, I could attribute that to having poor social skills instead of a disorder. I realized my problem was that I was self-diagnosing myself based on the list of symptoms I read. The problem lies in the fact that the list of symptoms is usually presented in subjective terms that can be understood in many different ways. I continually looked at the relevant cases in an extreme context, which made me more likely to see myself as someone who had social anxiety.

I also realized that when I started this research, I was still adjusting to the new life that college students face. I was constantly meeting new people and was around new social situations that could be nerve-racking to anybody. Now that it is later in the semester, I feel I have a better handle on social interactions. I also came to the realization that the reason I wasn't socializing as much as others wasn't because I was embarrassed, I just didn't know what to say. I always felt awkward because I knew I should say something, but nothing would come to my mind. It wasn't because I worried about what others would think. I could narrow my problems down to poor social skills instead of social anxiety disorder.

I learned a lot throughout my search about social anxiety disorder. While I never did find out if I have social anxiety disorder, I have regained hope that I can get through my socializing problems. While

I no longer worry so much about whether or not I have a problem, I plan to read the book by Schneier and Welkowitz in its entirety to get a better grasp on ways to enhance my social skills. Since it seems I do not need professional help, I am confident that I will overcome my problems with social situations.

Works Cited

Beidel, Deborah C., and Samuel M. Turner. *Shy Children, Phobic Adults: Nature and Treatment of Social Phobia.* Washington, DC: American Psychological Association, 1998.

Craske, Michelle G. *Anxiety Disorders: Psychological Approaches to Theory and Treatment.* Boulder, CO: Westview Press, 1999.

Greiner, Doug. Personal Interview. 18 Oct. 2006.

Myers, David G. *Psychology.* 8th ed. New York: Worth Publishers, 2006.

Muller, Jacqueline E., Liezl Koen, Soraya Seedat, and Dan J. Stein. "Social Anxiety Disorder: Current Treatment Recommendations." *CNS Drugs.* 19: 5 (2005): 377–391. *PsychInfo.* EBSCOhost. Missouri State University, Springfield, MO. 18 Oct. 2006. <http://web.ebscohost.com>.

National Institute of Mental Health. *A Real Illness: Social Phobia.* Bethesda, MD: National Institute of Mental Health. No date.

- - -. *Facts About Social Phobia.* Bethesda, Maryland: National Institute of Mental Health: 1999.

Schneier, Franklin, and Lawrence Welkowitz. *The Hidden Face of Shyness: Understanding and Overcoming Social Anxiety.* New York: Avon Books, 1996.

Tillfors, Maria. "Why Do Some Individuals Develop Social Phobia? A Review with Emphasis on the Neurobiological Influences." *Nordic Journal of Psychiatry.* 58: 4 (2004): 267–276. *PsychInfo.* EBSCOhost. Missouri State University, Springfield, MO. 18 Oct. 2006. <http://web.ebscohost.com>.

"We're Sick of Being Shy." *The Times (UK).* Feb. 2006: 4. *Newspaper Source.* EBSCOhost. Missouri State University, Springfield, MO. 4 Dec. 2006. <http://web.ebscohost.com>.

A Child's Need for Universal Healthcare

Chris Witt

> This essay was written as a position paper assignment for Writing
> II: Academic Writing. It uses CSE style.

Abstract

HEALTHCARE HAS ALWAYS BEEN a problem for certain people in
Missouri. Those people would be the uninsured, or more specifically,
the uninsured children of Missouri. These children cannot pick a job
based on insurance plans. These children are not responsible for their
lifestyles or their checkbooks, yet these children are being punished by
not having coverage from a healthcare provider. Universal healthcare
is an idea that has been debated for many years. Some people believe
that healthcare is not the responsibility of the government. Other
people believe that healthcare is a right, not a privilege. For children,
healthcare is a necessity, and many of these children are not receiving
medical care because they are not insured.

Introduction

IF MISSOURI STATE UNIVERSITY (MSU) had six times the amount of
students on campus, there would be over 110,000 students cramming
the halls and flooding the sidewalks between each class. Although
that might be hard to picture, an even more difficult thought for me
to fathom is if all 110,000 students were children under eighteen. If
MSU had a campus large enough to house all of these children, then
it still wouldn't be capable of accommodating the 121,000 uninsured
children in Missouri.[1] These children do not have scheduled
checkups with their doctor every year, they do not receive all of the
medication that they need, and they do not always receive proper
treatment because they are uninsured. The type of healthcare
program that would be the most beneficial for uninsured children
under eighteen is universal healthcare. Universal healthcare for
children under eighteen would be a valuable healthcare program for
the children in Missouri who are not currently covered by health
insurance and, therefore, are not receiving the treatment they may
need.

Background

ONE OF THE MAJOR FACTORS for the large number of uninsured children in Missouri is the number of children living in homes that are in poverty. In 2003, 19.6% of Missouri's children under the age of five and 14.9% of children ages 5–17 lived in poverty.[2] The federal poverty level for a family of four is $18,850.[2] The Missouri Department of Economic Development reports that a family of four needs between $28,000 and $39,000 to meet essential needs. These families that are living in poverty are $10,000 below the level that the state sets for only essential needs. These essential needs are food, shelter, and clothing. If these families are $10,000 short of meeting these immediate needs, how are they going to be capable of providing health insurance for their children?

One of the reasons for children living in poverty is because the parents do not have the proper education for higher paying jobs. In Missouri, one out of every five births is to a mother without a high school diploma.[2] The national average salary for a worker without a high school diploma is $18,734.[3] This means that, on the average, one out of every five children is born into poverty. Even if a child is born into a family with parents who have received a high school diploma or higher, there are still 22% of those children living in families that receive food stamps.[2] These families, those that need help paying for necessary groceries, are the same families that need help paying for necessary healthcare.

One of the largest problems with children being uninsured is the fact that they might not see a doctor on a regular basis or if they are sick. This is because the parents do not have the money for a doctor or an emergency room visit. In America, almost 33% of uninsured children did not see a doctor in 2005. In the same year, 88% of children with insurance visited a doctor.[4] The amount of visits to the hospital by children covered by insurance was twice that of uninsured children. The children that are not visiting a doctor are the ones that are missing school because they are sick. They don't have the insurance to pay for prescription drugs for faster recovery, and the parents are missing work or, even worse, leaving their sick child home alone so they do not miss any more work. These families that live in poverty are the ones that have the most need for a healthcare program that can help and even save the lives of their children. This type of healthcare program should be provided without charge to the families that support these children.

Discussion

THE BASIC IDEA FOR UNIVERSAL healthcare is that taxpayers and private contributions would help pay for healthcare no matter the patient's financial status. The type of universal healthcare that would be most beneficial to Missouri's children would be a type of healthcare that allows children under eighteen to be covered if their parents are not receiving healthcare packages from their employers. This could cover basic checkups for children during flu season or even pay for a life-saving operation for a newborn that wouldn't have a chance otherwise because the parents or parent does not have the money to cover the operation.

Many people believe that universal healthcare is too expensive for everyone else. It is true that universal healthcare is an expense to everyone; universal healthcare is a universal effort. The average cost of healthcare for a child in Missouri is $121 per month.[5] With 121,000 uninsured children in Missouri, this equals $14,641,000 per month to cover these children. According to the U.S. Census Bureau, the estimated population of taxpayers in Missouri in 2005 was 4,408,236.[6] Therefore the cost to each taxpayer would be a little more than $3 per month. This figure is if only taxpayers paid the cost for universal healthcare. Most countries with this type of healthcare also have private donations and federal spending to lower the cost to the taxpayers.

A type of universal healthcare for uninsured children is already in effect in Illinois, a model state that can be reveal lessons learned. Illinois has a program called *All Kids* that allows families below the poverty line to have free child healthcare.[7] Families that make more than the poverty line but still are unable to afford healthcare for multiple children have a low monthly charge. For example, if a single mother makes $20,000 a year she is above the federal poverty line, but what if she is still unable to make expensive healthcare payments for her child? Under *All Kids*, her payment would cost only $15 per month to fully cover her child. Although technically this model is not universal healthcare, it is a great start that is getting praise from other states looking for a way to have healthcare coverage for all of their children.

Many people believe that healthcare is not the government's responsibility and that healthcare is not a right. Healthcare may not be the responsibility of the government, but the government has already shown that the children of America are their responsibility. The "No Child Left Behind Act" passed in 2001 is a program that puts accountability on teachers for educating children so that in the 2012–2014 school year the children of America will be at a proficient level. Over the last three years the federal government has given 72.5 billion dollars for this act.[8] This finding shows that children are important to our government. There is no better way to have the children reach a proficient level in school than to keep them healthy and able to attend school.

Another argument against universal healthcare is that people who take care of themselves and are healthy should not have to pay for the people who are unhealthy because of their way of life: for example, smoking, obesity, or drugs. For most children under age eighteen, the repercussions of these acts are not yet medically present if they are living that lifestyle; therefore, people are not paying for other people's mistakes or bad choices.

Another argument is that universal healthcare would remove the right to privacy between doctors and patients because the government would demand power to oversee the health of the patient. This might sound like another "Big Brother" conspiracy, but I believe that having a centralized database for patients' medical histories available at all hospitals would greatly increase the efficiency of obtaining the background information for all patients, no matter which hospital provided their medical care. This would decrease initial paperwork and initial waiting time during the first critical minutes a patient arrives for treatment.

Hospitals have become such a big business that there are multiple cases of private hospitals not admitting patients because they did not have insurance to cover the cost of care. With universal healthcare, this refusal to see patients could never happen again. The private hospitals could treat children without sending them to a public hospital.

Another argument against universal healthcare is that hospitals would be more crowded for emergency care because of the free medical treatment. Hospitals that are overpopulated are the public hospitals that provide Medicaid. If universal healthcare was available for children, then it wouldn't matter which hospital the child visited. This would mean a lower population for the public hospitals that are already exceeding their patient capacity.

The amount of time for treatment is a question that has been asked about universal healthcare. In 1993, the average wait for medical treatment in Canada was 9.3 weeks. This figure comes from before Canada adopted universal healthcare. In 2001, after Canada began universal healthcare, the average wait for medical treatment was 16.5 weeks.[9] This is a 77% increase, but this also means that 100% of the patients were treated. Although children in Missouri might have to wait longer for non-critical treatment, universal healthcare would allow these children the treatment they might not have received without universal healthcare.

Conclusion

CHILDREN IN MISSOURI NEED healthcare; there are over 121,000 children in Missouri not receiving healthcare. People in Missouri can make a difference for these children. These children are the same children that the government said would not be left behind in education. Why are they being left behind in healthcare? The reason why most children are not covered by health insurance is because they are living in poverty. Universal healthcare for children under eighteen, who are not covered by their parents' insurance, would be the best way to insure these children. With little more than $3 from each taxpayer a month, which could be substantially less with private and government contributions, each child in Missouri could have access to free visits to the doctor, free medicine, and free treatment that every child deserves.

References

[1] Families USA Report on Uninsured Children [Internet]. (MO): Citizens for Missouri's Children; 2006 [cited 2006 Nov 20]. Available from: http://www.mokids.org/library/FamiliesUSAUninsuredKidsReport.cfm
[2] The State of Missouri's Children: 2006 [Internet]. (MO): Center for Family Policy and Research; 2006 [cited 2006 Nov 20]. Available from: http://www.missouri.edu/~cfprwww/Mochildren06.pdf

[3] Back to School; U.S. Census [Internet]. Kansas City (MO); Kansas City Info Zine; [2006 Aug 28; cited 2006 Nov 20]. Available from: http://www.infozine.com/news/stories/op/storiesView/sid/17334/

[4] Many Uninsured Kids Going Without Healthcare [Internet]. [place unknown]: Daily News Central; [2005 Aug 2; cited 2006 Nov 22]. Available from: http://health.dailynewscentral.com/content/view/0001411/39/

[5] Medicaid in Missouri [Internet]. Columbia (MO); The Center for Health Policy; [2003 June; cited 2006 Nov 22]. Available from: http://healthpolicy.missouri.edu/factsheets/momedicaid.pdf

[6] State and County Quick Facts [Internet]. [place unknown]: U.S. Census Bureau; c2006 [updated 8 June 2006; cited 2006 Nov 20]. Available from: http://quickfacts.census.gov/qfd/states/29000.html

[7] Mantone, Joseph. Stating the Case for Coverage. Modern Healthcare 2006 May; 36(18): 6–9. In: Academic Search Premier database on the Internet]. Springfield (MO): EBSCO Host c2006 [cited 2006 Nov 20]. [about 35 paragraphs]. Available from: http://web.ebscohost.com; Article: 20877950.

[8] What the No Child Left Behind Law Means for Your Child [Internet]. (CA); Great Schools, c2006 [updated 2006 Sept; cited 2006 Nov 22]. Available from: http://www.greatschools.net/cgi-bin/showarticle/CA/205

[9] Benko, Laura B. Universal Appeal. Modern Healthcare 2003 April;33(15): 26-9. In: Academic Search Premier [database on the internet]. Springfield (MO): EBSCO Host c2006 [cited 2006 Nov 20]. [about 30 paragraphs]. Available from: http://web.ebscohost.com; Article: 9608299.

American Male Malaise in Fight Club

Eric Hartman

> This essay was written as a position paper assignment for Writing II: Academic Writing.

IN RECENT YEARS, A CRISIS of sorts has come about in America. This is not a crisis that has always warranted attention, mostly because it is based on the notion of American men suffering, though not in a physical sense, but rather a psychological sense. The problem, often called "Masculinity in Crisis," refers to men feeling emasculated by their culture. Of course, there are several critiques of what exactly lays behind these feelings. Since film and other forms of art can reflect what is happening in our culture and open discussion about different issues, it is important to look at the masculinity crisis through film. One film in particular, *Fight Club*, based on the book by Chuck Palahniuk, focuses on men and their issues of masculinity. A thorough look into *Fight Club* can reveal several factors behind this crisis. By examining the issues it raises, perhaps conclusions can be drawn to provide insight into this malaise of the American male.

Before beginning any in-depth discussion of the situation, an overview of *Fight Club* is necessary. The film follows the story of the nameless narrator, often referred to as "Jack" due to the medical stories he reads in a scene that personify the various body parts of a man named Jack. Jack is miserable working at his corporate job at an unnamed car company and living his life as a consumer. He develops insomnia and can only sleep after he connects emotionally with strangers at different support groups for diseases he does not have. But once he meets Marla, another "faker" like himself who attends various support groups just for thrills, he can no longer cry and therefore can no longer sleep. During a business meeting, Jack meets a soap salesman named Tyler Durden, who gives Jack his card. When Jack's condo unexpectedly explodes, he calls on this same Tyler Durden for help. After discussing their problems in a bar, Tyler confronts Jack, forcing Jack to ask if he can stay at his place. When Jack complies, Tyler says, "I want you to hit me as hard as you can." So Jack hits Tyler, Tyler punches Jack back, and they have a revelation, learning something about themselves from the encounter.

As the two men live in squalor at Tyler's house, they also begin a "fight club" in the basement of a bar. This club draws men from all over to come and fight and feel alive. Meanwhile, Tyler has started a sexual relationship with Marla the "faker," much to Jack's resentment.

Fight clubs soon start springing up in major cities across the U.S. The clubs escalate into Project Mayhem, which at first is a series of pranks against corporate and capitalist symbols, but devolves into full-fledged terrorism. Under Tyler Durden's leadership, the members of Project Mayhem plant explosives in credit card buildings in hopes everyone will return to economic equality. Jack realizes what Tyler is doing and tries to stop him; however, on his quest to stop Tyler, Jack begins to realize that he and Tyler are actually the same person. Jack also discovers that while he has been Tyler, he has made certain there was no way for him to stop the imminent explosion.

Confronting his alter ego in one of the last scenes, he realizes the only way to get rid of Tyler is to kill himself. Shooting himself in the mouth, Jack kills his Tyler persona but is not himself killed. Marla joins him as the buildings crumble, and he turns to her and says, "Everything is going to be fine. You met me at a very strange time in my life," thus concluding the movie.

The source of male malaise is often credited to the switch in American culture from men working in utilitarian jobs producing materials to a consumer economy. In Susan Faludi's epic book, *Stiffed: The Betrayal of the American Man* chronicling six years of interviews and research into the crisis of manhood, she describes the post-World War II promise fathers made to their sons at "the moment of America's great bounty and ascendance" (597). Faludi claims, "Implicit in all of this was a promise of loyalty, a guarantee to the new man of tomorrow that his company would never fire him, his wife would never leave him, and the team he rooted for would never pull up stakes" (27). The promise was that if a man was loyal and worked hard, he would be successful on the job and at home. But with the switch to a consumer economy, men no longer felt useful, because "however little control old-fashioned factory workers had over company policy, they at least knew that their work was tangible" (Faludi 79). As noted in *Stiffed*, the corporate world became a site of malaise, because men "sensed all control rested in the hands of faceless authorities" (80). Like these men,

Jack works as a recall coordinator in the corporate world of automobile manufacturing.

No longer feeling useful in their corporate jobs, men transferred the former ideal of hard work and its tangible results into purchasing products. Looking at the article "Surviving American Culture: On Chuck Palahniuk," Eduardo Mendieta assesses this idea: "Mass culture liberated us from culture by making of each one of us its consumer, and through consumption its producers" (398). In *Fight Club*, Jack claims he "became a slave to the IKEA nesting instinct," as furniture, prices, and product descriptions pop up all over his apartment, rendering it into a catalogue of sorts. Making note of this fact in "Virtual Violence in *Fight Club*: This is What Transformation of Masculine Ego Feels Like," Terry Lee says, "Men (and women) want things because the free enterprise, consumer-materialist culture they live in benefits from their desiring things" (419). Lee even goes on to claim Jack "substitutes a desire for consumer products for sexual desire and for emotional connection to human beings" and "obsesses over his domestic sphere and its furnishings" (419). This obsession is part of "gender role strain" where men "necessarily fail as they try to live up to the culture's measure of masculinity" (Lee 419). On this reading, there are so many contradictory roles for men to fill in modern culture that they begin to think it is impossible for them to do so, and as a result they "feel always inferior, feel like they come up short of meeting the cultural fathers' expectations" (Lee 419). In this way, men have come to feel emasculated by their very culture, a culture based on consumerism and materialism.

Related to the problems of consumerism and materialism is the "ornamental" culture, which Faludi concludes is ultimately the problem of masculinity. She claims men can only partake of this ornamental culture by shopping and "displaying prettiness," which tradition has held as feminine (602). In present American culture these feminine qualities are a definite part of consumerism, but ornamental culture is even more encompassing because "even the most traditional of craftsmen and community builders lived in a world where personal worth was judged in ornamental terms: Were they 'sexy'? Were they 'known'? Had they 'won'?" (598). Prior to the modern culture, winning was important in that it helped society. Winning men "strived and wrangled to wrest a community out of wilderness; they 'won the West' to build a nation" (598). But present society "elevated winning to the very apex of manhood while at the same time disconnecting it from social purpose. Being first seemed to be all that mattered" (598). Winning for the sake of being first represents the notion that the culture has come to care only about image without any concern for social value.

Examining the "ornamental" problem in *Fight Club* can lead to several conclusions. It can be said that Jack lives according to the standards of the ornamental world, as he makes purchase after purchase of IKEA products. This factor is especially pronounced when he asks, "What sort of furniture defines me as a person?" He is heavily concerned with his image, especially after his condo explodes and his possessions are destroyed. He explains his loss to Tyler, "I had it all. I had a stereo that was very decent, a wardrobe that was getting very respectable. I was close to being complete." Tyler responds with, "We're consumers. We're byproducts of a lifestyle obsession. Murder, crime, poverty—these things don't concern me. What concerns me are celebrity magazines, television with 500 channels, some guy's name on my underwear. Rogaine, Viagra, Olestra…" This exchange is surely an indictment of ornamental culture.

Only after living with Tyler, the epitome of the hyper-masculine male, in a house devoid of image or superficiality—in a word, a dump—does Jack begin to lose the feminine instincts he had come to adopt. Jack and Tyler separate themselves from the ornamental culture and through this they create Fight Club. Tyler eventually expresses his frustration of the ornamental in a speech to the members of Fight Club:

> Man, I see in Fight Club the strongest and smartest men who've ever lived. I see all this potential. And I see it squandered. God damn it. An entire generation pumping gas, waiting tables, slaves with white collars. Advertising has its taste in cars and clothes, working jobs we hate so we can buy shit we don't need. We're the middle children of history, man. No purpose or place. We have no Great War, no Great Depression. Our Great War's a spiritual war. Our Great Depression is our lives. We've all been raised on television to believe that one day we would all be millionaires, movie

gods, and rock stars. But we won't. We are slowly learning that fact. And we're very, very pissed off.

Durden's speech echoes so many of the problems of ornamental culture. Once Fight Club evolves into Project Mayhem, Tyler tells the men, "You are not unique snowflakes." In fact, Tyler removes their names as part of Project Mayhem. This is designed to make everyone equal and so that no one stands out.

It is important to note that Tyler Durden may ultimately represent the ornamental for Jack. When Tyler confronts Jack and tells him they are the same person, Tyler says to Jack, "All the ways you wish you could be, and that's me. I look like you want to look, I fuck like you want to fuck." Jack himself is recognized by all members of Fight Club as Tyler Durden when he travels from town to town trying to thwart his alter ego's destructive plans. Tyler Durden is celebrated above the rest. He would be the opposite of what he tells the men:

> You are not special. You are not a beautiful or unique snowflake. You are the same decaying organic matter as everything else. We are the all-singing, all-dancing crap of the world.

Because he has started Fight Club, because he has created Project Mayhem, and because he is the organizer and leader of it all, Tyler Durden is special and unique. Who could be a better representation of the ornamental than Tyler Durden, particularly when he is played by Hollywood's perennial pretty boy, Brad Pitt?

Not only does he have the look of a celebrity, Tyler also shows the aggressiveness associated with the constant need to win. In her article "The Masculinity Muddle," Marnie Ko quotes psychologist Wade Horn: "Confusion about their masculinity leaves young men with little choice but aggression to prove their masculinity" (41). Tyler and the rest of the men of Fight Club feel alive because they are finally able to demonstrate their long lost masculinity. As Mendieta suggests, their "quest for viable masculinity ends up re-enacting the very rituals that have eviscerated masculinity in the first place: misogyny, militarism, bullying, terrorism, and gratuitous violence" (397). For Jack, Tyler becomes the very thing he does not want to be, and he pushes himself to put a stop to it.

This theory of the consumerist and ornamental culture has its detractors of course. Joel Stein denies it entirely in the *Newsweek* article "The Emasculation Proclamation," saying:

> Men are fine. We don't want to go back to construction with other men, mostly because construction is hard. . . . We're not men like our fathers: confident, stern, and single-handedly supporting a family. But we're happier and more pleasant in our permanent adolescence reading *Maxim* and watching *The Man Show*. It definitely beats going to war. (46)

Then there is the theory that men are only looking to portray themselves as victims. Lynn M. Ta begins her article "Hurt So Good: *Fight Club*, Masculine Violence, and the Crisis of Capitalism" with the idea of the masochist who developed in American society, an idea she admits is borrowed heavily from David Savran's book *Taking It Like a Man*. In America and a large part of Western culture, the concepts of liberalism and capitalism gave rise to a "new self-regulating subject" who is the same as "the masochistic subject who, perceiving himself to be solely responsible for his successes and failures, must discipline and torture himself, not only as a means of thriving, but as an assertion of self" (Ta 269). This "capitalistic masochism where masculinity could be asserted through hard work and self-denial" was a product of previous eras (275). This model fits with the masculinity of old. She compares the "capitalistic masochism" to masochism in Freud's work, described as a condition where "the individual's internalization of authority, such as the Law or the Parents, results in the superego's disciplining and punishment of the ego" (269). While the masochist remains complacent and unable to act because of this "internalization," the white male rebel, a Savran notion developing as a result of the many movements of the 1960s and 1970s, can no longer stand being dominated in a culture that has emasculated him. Without the power to actually change anything, the rebel "seeks recourse in victimhood, becoming the divided self who at once laments his victimization but also depends on it as a point of protest and identification" (269–270).

Interestingly, the white male rebel is also incapable of acting to relieve his malaise. Sally Robinson, an ardent feminist, addresses her interpretation of white male victimhood in "Putting the Stud Back into Gender Studies," which is not so much an academic discussion but a critique of *Stiffed* and *Fight Club*, as well as a plug for her own book *Marked Men*. Having done research for her book, Robinson is qualified to discuss the material. She asserts that claiming victimhood and identifying a masculinity crisis is a way for men "to reoccupy the centre of cultural priority, value and interest" and "seek new routes to power" (VII). This power and attention seemingly has been turned over to women.

Faludi acknowledges that men have always needed a clear enemy to fight and define their masculinity. The finger-pointing was a way to establish an enemy, such as "scheming feminists, affirmative-action proponents, job-grabbing illegal aliens, the wife of a president" (604). Having someone to blame would make these men victims of something. Robinson criticizes Faludi for failing "to entertain the possibility that men might take pleasure in becoming 'ornamental,' that men might be liberated by giving up a utilitarian, producer masculinity that has no place in a post-industrial economy" (VII). She says *Stiffed* also fails "to listen for the possibility that being 'ornamental' does not necessarily mean being 'feminized'" (VII). But Robinson appears to have missed the part in *Stiffed* where Faludi says women have been victimized by "ornamental" culture as well, stating, "Men and women both feel cheated of lives in which they might have contributed to a social world" (602).

The Women's Movement of the 1960s and 1970s came about because women were no longer satisfied with being housewives whose only power came from shopping and vanity, or "power at the point of purchase," as Faludi quotes from Betty Friedan's 1963 book *The Feminine Mystique* (601). Though Robinson may have a point that some men would enjoy being "ornamental," Faludi's numerous interview subjects attest that they are not happy about being on display and having to be a star or famous to be viewed as successful. Ta does not let men off the hook: she suggests that "sitting at the top of the social and economic pecking order, they are ones who have allowed masculinity to be commodified" (267).

Addressing this problem in the context of needing an enemy, Faludi says, "Men have no clearly defined enemy who is oppressing them" (604). She further asks, "How can men be oppressed when the culture has already identified them as the oppressors, and when they see themselves that way?" (604). Men need something besides victimhood and someone to battle. Faludi suggests that the old paradigm be taken down, since, as feminists have discovered now that they have gained power, it no longer works; the "problems persist" (604). In the end, it is not about being a victim: Faludi wants men to forget about winning and being a man, and try to be human (607). Yet, according to Ta, the victim element of masculinity is evident in *Fight Club*. The men in *Fight Club* can be seen as both aggressors and as victims. They fight like men but receive like women. When the audience discovers that Jack and Tyler are the same person, the victim (Jack) and aggressor (Tyler) theme comes into play again, as well as the argument of masochism (Ta 273).

Acknowledging that "there are bigger problems in the world," Christopher M. Duncan says in his article "Liberalism and the Challenge of *Fight Club*: Notes Toward an American Theory of the Good Life" that "the middle children of history . . . represent an important problem for liberalism and American society and a challenge to American political thinkers and theorists" (136). Duncan's article presents an almost stand-alone argument of the crisis that begins with the formation of liberalism and how it once used to guide people. According to him, traditional liberalism accepts all ways of life, but believes that certain ways of living are better than others (127). Liberalism can and should be seen in a way to make young people understand the importance of the examined life. Duncan posits that American society has developed into one where the claim that the "unexamined life *is* worth living" is seriously considered (134). But this cannot be true, because "happiness depends on the dialogic search itself" (133). Duncan proposes that liberalism must guide the "plebicians," or those who are "plebeian or commoner in taste and sentiment and patrician or aristocratic in means and opportunity" (120). These are the types Durden describes as "the middle children of history" who can do almost anything they want, but either do not know what they want to do or choose not to do it. By Duncan's definition of liberalism, it is up to the culture to direct these lost people back to the pursuit of happiness by "dialogic or sermonic prodding toward a richer more fulfilling diet," because otherwise "America will continue to eat only the thinnish gruel of bourgeois life" (139). In sum, he wants Americans to "live deliberately" (139).

The problem with *Fight Club*, by Duncan's assertion, is that it "has taken a side, but not a position. We know what Jack (and *Fight Club*) is against, but we do not know what he is for. As such, he is both a product of contemporary liberalism's failure and a co-conspirator in its continued demise" (136). Jack is against the "'bourgeouisfication' of American culture" that "has failed to create the happiness of liberalism" (137). Duncan criticizes the movie heavily for failing to offer a reasonable solution, and that point is open to debate. Oddly enough, Tyler Durden does intervene in the life of one young man in the film. By pointing the gun at the head of Raymond K. Hessel, a clerk at a convenience store, Tyler forces Raymond to confess what he actually wanted to do with his life. Raymond says he wanted to be a veterinarian, and Tyler instructs him to begin working toward that goal or else he will kill him. This example could represent what Duncan has proposed liberalism should be doing, but obviously not by employing such violent measures.

The masculinity crisis has several possible causes, but what of the solutions? Aside from Christopher M. Duncan's argument, which is almost unrelated to the rest, the arguments all point toward a common goal. Since Duncan's theory of the problem and his own solution for it have already been presented, the common solution of the others remains. Lynn M. Ta throws in her opinion that fighting consumerism is not the answer, but "abandoning" it could be (276). For Susan Faludi, there is a unified struggle against the ornamental, because, as she says in *Stiffed*, "Social responsibility is not the special province of masculinity; it's the lifelong work of all citizens in a community where people are knit together by meaningful and mutual concerns" (607). Men and women working alongside each other for a greater good instead of competing for image is Faludi's solution to the masculinity crisis. Lee feels that "virtual violence" or "violence that can be productive, useful to man" as "enacted in myth, story, and film" (420), could be the solution. Lee further states, "The film's violence is a projected picture of the 'virtual violence' that one can enact within the psyche to destroy harmful gender-role paradigms to make room for healthier masculinities" (423). Eduardo Mendieta proposes that "Tyler Durden is the alter ego that men must exorcise. Men must free themselves from the ghosts of a masculine Olympus, whose only existence is to vitiate any feasible and realistic sense of maleness" (397).

In *Fight Club*, Jack exorcises Tyler Durden in the end by shooting himself in the face. Viewing Jack as the emasculated, unhappy male and Tyler as the hyper masculine image of old that no longer fits in modern society, perhaps the Jack that has known Tyler Durden and ousted him can be seen as the new man. In her review of the film, "It's *Thelma & Louise* for Guys," Faludi points out that *Fight Club* "renounces even the violence its lead character is drawn to" and "the adolescent fraternity" (89). Faludi emphasizes that in the end Jack "throws his lot in with the defiant, if deviant, woman" and "seems poised to finally begin life as an adult man" (89). Jack does not want to show his angst by blowing up buildings. He decides to forge ahead as a full human being and not some partial notion of manhood. In other words, there can be a rejection of the culture's obsession with image and aggressive winning in the pursuit of happiness and success. Consumerism does not have to be the dominating force that it is. By teaming together, perhaps men and women can create a solution to the culture by working toward common goals that have societal value, discussing and negotiating the ways to true happiness, as we may hope was the case with Jack and Marla.

Works Cited

Duncan, Christopher M. "Liberalism and the Challenge of *Fight Club*: Notes Toward an American Theory of the Good Life." *disClosure* 12 (2003): 119–144.

Faludi, Susan. "It's *Thelma & Louise* for Guys." *Newsweek* 25 Oct. 1999: 89.

- - -. *Stiffed: the Betrayal of the American Man*. New York: W. Morrow and Co., 1999.

Fight Club. Dir. David Fincher. Perf. Brad Pitt, Edward Norton, and Helena Bonham Carter. 20th Century Fox, 1999.

Ko, Marnie. "The Masculinity Muddle." *Report/Newsmagazine* 22 Nov. 1999: 1.

Lee, Terry. "Virtual Violence in *Fight Club*: This is What Transformation of Masculine Ego Feels Like." *Journal of American & Comparative Cultures* 25.3/4 (2002): 418–423.

Mendieta, Eduardo. "Surviving American Culture: On Chuck Palahniuk." *Philosophy and Literature* 29.2 (2005): 394–408.

Robinson, Sally. "Putting the Stud Back into Gender Studies." *Times Higher Education Supplement* 15 Dec. 2000: vi–vii.

Stein, Joel. "The Emasculation Proclamation." *Time* 25 Oct. 1999: 46–49.

Ta, Lynn M. "Hurt So Good: *Fight Club*, Masculine Violence, and the Crisis of Capitalism." *Journal of American Culture* 29.3 (2006): 265–277.

Ein Finsteres Vermächtnis: *The Connection Between 19th Century Colonialism and the Nazi Regime*

Sean A. Wempe

> This research paper was written as a position paper for Writing II: Writing for Graduate and Professional Schools. It uses CMS.

Introduction: The Lost Pages of History

TYPICALLY, WHEN AN ANALYSIS of the Colonial Era and its impact is made, the examples that are focused on are those of British and French colonialism. This is understandable, since they were the power players who formed empires and commonwealths that endured for generation after generation, but there were others on the colonial scene that tend to be forgotten, particularly the relatively short appearance of Germany on the stage of colonial endeavors. Historians and laity alike often fall into the mental trap of regarding 19th century German colonialism as a failure, a mere outcropping of Bismarckian Imperialism that was ill-fated and short-lived. Such a view, however, ignores the great impact that German colonialism had, not only in shaping the history of those continents and islands that witnessed its colonial presence, but also on the German nation itself. As a result, there is simply not enough analysis of this topic that would seem to have much relevance to any complete understanding of Germany's history. Luckily, some scholars are now beginning to explore this previously neglected period in Germany's past and are finding more and more connections between this era and the mentalities and policies of later portions of German history and Western civilization as a whole. Germany's brief ascendancy during the colonial period had a profound impact not only on its colonies, but also Germany itself, altering the nation's view of itself and its relation to others, creating a German "colonial mentality" that was to have notable influence during the Nazi regime.

Ein Riesiges Reich: The Extent of Germany's Original Colonial Empire

IN ORDER TO FULLY UNDERSTAND the level of an impact colonialism had on Germany's sense of identity, one must first understand how deeply it became involved in building a *Kolonialreich* in its brief interlude in this era of world history. Though many don't know it, from 1881, when Bismarck gave into interest groups pressuring for colonies, to 1914, when the nation lost them to the Allies, Germany constructed and controlled the third largest colonial empire in the world, bested only by England and France.[1] This empire was extremely diversified, with the Germans holding sway over numerous islands in the Pacific, as well as controlling a large section of Africa, including modern-day Namibia, Togo, the Cameroons, and Tanzania, that extended over a 900,000 square mile portion of the globe, "four times the area of the [European] Reich."[2] Such a large sphere of influence certainly exemplified Bismarck's concept of the Balance of Power between the great nations of Europe, giving Germany relatively equal political clout with the giants of England and France.

The Germans were also not passive landlords of their colonies. They invested heavily, morally, and monetarily, into what they viewed as their portion of "The White Man's Burden" to civilize the more primitive nations of the world, and were praised by their colonial contemporaries. And, in fact, they did bring many positives to the world colonial stage.[3] They introduced Western technology and philosophies to Africa, including the two-sided sword of ethnography, constructed dock yards and roads, and laid some 4,500 kilometers of railway track to facilitate industry and transport within their colonies.[4] In terms of what they brought back to Europe from their colonies, the Germans were pioneers

---

[1] Blackshire-Belay, Carol Aisha. "German Imperialism in Africa: The Distorted Images of Cameroon, Namibia, Tanzania, and Togo." *Journal of Black Studies* 23, no. 2 (1992): 235–46. http://links.jstor.org, p. 235, 238.

[2] Ibid, p. 238.

[3] The negative impacts of German colonization on the world, of which there are many, will be discussed later in this paper, as the positives are important in trying to understand the German Colonial psyche that was created, which will also be discussed.

[4] Ibid, p. 237.

in the study of African languages, and also produced African scholars, such as Anton Wilhelm Amo, who enriched European philosophy by offering different perspectives.[5] Germany was certainly becoming a colonial powerhouse, investing more, and, though entering late to the colonial scene, quickly outstripping its contemporaries in development and management of its colonies.

Der Kolonialgeist: Germany's Colonial Mindset

GIVEN HOW HEAVILY Germany invested in its colonies, and as dependent as it became on the possession of such colonies for national grandeur mimicking the other great nations of Europe, it is no wonder that the German population felt a profound sense of loss, materially and ideologically, when the Allies stripped it of its satellites at the end of the First World War. From this loss and humiliation, a sentiment of desire to return to colonial grandeur arose, adding to the formation of Germany's dangerous preoccupation with restitution for the injustices that had been inflicted on it by the Allies.

As early as 1918, special interest groups, such as the *Reichsbund der Kolonialdeutschen (RBKD)* and the extremely influential *Deutsche Kolonialgesellschaft (DKG)*, were formed by those Germans who had lost homes, property, or positions of power through the loss of the colonies.[6] These numerous "colonial clubs" that arose following the stripping of Germany's colonies after the First World War were composed of elite individuals of a very conservative mentality and constituted only a small fraction of the society, but had a large political voice and represented Germany's desire to return to glory. By May of 1930, a conference of former colonial ministers was agitating the Weimar Republic to regain Germany's colonies with a list of seven guidelines, outlining such expectations as equal rights for Germans everywhere, protection of the German culture abroad, an understanding worldwide that some of Germany's colonies were not ready to be independent (coupled with a desire to see increased efforts and propaganda for the German government to acquire mandates), and, most importantly, a renunciation of the "Colonial Guilt Lie," a not-wholly unjustified statement made by the Allies that the Germans

---

[5] Ibid, p. 237.

[6] Schmokel, Wolfe W. *Dream of Empire: German Colonialism, 1919–1945*. London: Yale University Press, 1964, p. 2.

had been poor colonial administrators who had violently abused their colonial subjects.[7]

Dr. Heinrich Schnee, former governor of German East Africa (Tanganyika—modern day Tanzania), was not only at the head of the *DKG* and organizer of the conference of former ministers in 1930, but was also the most vehement advocate on the world stage for the return of Germany's former colonies.[8] In 1926, Dr. Schnee wrote and published a protest called *German Colonization: Past and Future: The Truth About the German Colonies,* denouncing the "Colonial Guilt Lie" that he called a myth cooked up by the Allies to justify their control of Germany's former mandates.[9] In his argument throughout the book, he tries to refute this sentiment of Germany's "colonial guilt" by outlining his view of German administration in the colonies, the praise it received from other imperial nations when it entered the colonial arena, and the sentiments of the natives to the Germans as opposed to those nations who held those nations subsequently as mandates and protectorates.[10] Schnee also used Wilson's Fourteen Points to defend heavily the right of Germany to keep its colonies, citing Point Five[11] as his main argument: both Germany and its colonies were denied the right of self-determination by such actions, and the Allies acted selfishly in their own interests, in essence sentencing Germany and its colonies to ruin and thus should be responsible for rectifying this action by restoring Germany to its former glory.[12]

Schnee's work was obviously biased, but it well portrayed the sentiments and national attachments that a significant portion of the German population felt towards their colonies at the time and signifies the level of impact the loss of those colonies had on Germany

---

[7] Schmokel, p. 9.

[8] Ibid, p. 2–9.

[9] Schnee, Heinrich. *German Colonization Past and Future: The Truth About the German Colonies.* London: George Allen & Unwin Ltd, 1926, p. 62.

[10] Ibid, p. 62–73.

[11] "A free, open-minded, and absolutely impartial adjustment of all colonial claims, based upon a strict observance of the principle that in determining all such questions of sovereignty the interests of the populations concerned must have equal weight with the equitable claims of the government whose title is to be determined." —Woodrow Wilson; 8 January 1918.

[12] Schnee, p. 172–176.

economically and emotionally. This sentiment did not fall on deaf ears. Though it at first seemed focused on solely domestic and continental affairs, the Nazi party soon made appeals to this very affluent portion of the population by alluding to the possibility of reestablishing Germany's overseas empire. Political alliances were formed, and colonialism once again became a matter of importance to the German government once the Nazi regime firmly entrenched itself.[13]

Ein Finsteres Vermächtnis: The Dark Legacy Reapplied by the Nazi Regime

THE NAZIS FOUND THIS SENSE of injustice and the desire for restitution of the colonies a useful tool in their rise to power and expansion across Europe and North Africa, but that wasn't all that they tapped into from the colonial psyche. Hitler and his henchmen seem to have employed two much older, and far more horrible, elements of early German Colonialism to justify their actions at home and abroad—the concept of the "White Man's Burden" to civilize the world, and the atrocious tradition of mass genocide as a method to gain and maintain control of an area.

The Nazi party perpetuated the colonial concept of the "White Man's Burden," but did so in a way far removed from what the original colonizing powers had. While former colonial powers, including Germany, had viewed the continents of Africa, Asia, and America as uncivilized and in need of a sort of paternal aide and development, Nazi Germany applied this concept to their European neighbors: "For the Nazis, the acquisition of colonies outside of Europe took a backseat to [continental] expansion"[14] though they still needed to appease colonial tendencies and desire for economic gain. Upon an examination of the Nazi occupational policy and Aryanism, one can see that the entire campaign into Eastern Europe by the Nazis, on the grounds of *Lebensraum* and the sentiment that the Slavic nationalities were an inferior people, was more than just an occupation of foreign territory during a war, but was actually an

---

13 Schmokel, p. 18–45.

14 Poiger, Uta G. "Imperialism and Empire in Twentieth-Century Germany." *History and Memory* 17, no. 1/2 (2005): 117–43.

http://search.ebscohost.com/login (22 September 2006).

application of formal colonialism directed against fellow Europeans.[15] The Nazis built cities and railways while blatantly "disregarding indigenous settlements and economic structures"[16] in regions that they viewed as undeveloped *tabulae rasae*, moving in settlers and establishing new industries to replace "chaos" with "order."

However, a far more terrible legacy was carried on by the Nazis, not only in the newly conquered territories but also within the German state itself—mass extermination of entire groups, based on ethnicity, deemed a threat to the government's authority. In Nazi Germany, "the rise of Eugenics and a politics of dissimilation between Germans and those not considered German went hand in hand with increasing interconnections of metropole and colony. Germans linked belonging to the German nation with whiteness,"[17] continuing a viewpoint that had been true of German colonialists in Africa and Asia. This view of other races as inferior had, in the past, justified the mass extermination of numerous African tribes when they rebelled against colonial authority. The Herero and Nama of modern-day Namibia, the Abo and Bakoko of the Cameroons, the Konkomba of Togo, and most violently, the 250,000 to 300,000 Massai who were killed in the Maji-Maji rebellion of 1905 in Tanganyika are examples of tribes who were subjected to this horrible fate by the German colonial powers.[18] Some scholars argue that the Holocaust against the Jews and other "undesirables" by the Nazis was actually the final product of years of experimentation in genocide that had taken place in the colonies in Africa, asserting that those horrific "exterminatory wars" made the atrocities of the Nazi regime easier for the German populace to stomach, essentially normalizing mass extermination.[19] Once a group, such as the Jews or Slavs, had been labeled inferior, it seems natural that the same desensitized view that was directed against rebellious Africans would apply, the cries of those groups who were used as a

---

[15] Zimmerer, Jürgen. "The birth of the Ostland out of the spirit of colonialism: a postcolonial perspective on the Nazi policy of conquest and extermination." *Patterns of Prejudice* 39, no. 2 (2005): 197–219. http://search.ebscohost.com/login (22 September 2006): p. 202–204.

[16] Ibid. p. 204.

[17] Poiger, p. 120.

[18] Blackshire-Belay, p. 242.

[19] Zimmerer, p. 208–211.

scapegoat by the Nazis going unheard as they suffered the implementation of the "Final Solution" that had been used time and time before.

Conclusion: Research the Past to Understand the Present and to Possibly Foresee the Future

MORE SCHOLARSHIP MUST BE done on Germany's colonial period. Though Germany's ascendancy during the colonial period was brief, it affected how Germany viewed itself and had a profound impact on those nations it had once ruled, this "colonial mentality" horribly manifested during the Nazi regime. Further study of Bismarkian and Wilhelmine colonialism may not only shed light on this terrible time period of Germany's history, but may also prove an invaluable asset in understanding Cold-War and contemporary Germany as well. With Germany's growth as a political and economic rather than military dominance in the European Union, as well as its more recent pushes to gain veto authority in the United Nations, delving into the treasure trove of this now peaceful nation's colonial history would seem a worthwhile endeavor in order to better understand the force that might once again rise as one of the strongest powers in the world.

Bibliography

Blackshire-Belay, Carol Aisha. "German Imperialism in Africa: The Distorted Images of Cameroon, Namibia, Tanzania, and Togo." *Journal of Black Studies* 23, no. 2 (1992): 235–46. http://links.jstor.org (13 October 2006).

Poiger, Uta G. "Imperialism and Empire in Twentieth-Century Germany." *History and Memory* 17, no. 1/2 (2005): 117–43. http://search.ebscohost.com (22 September 2006).

Schmokel, Wolfe W. *Dream of Empire: German Colonialism, 1919-1945*. London: Yale, 1964.1– 45.

Schnee, Heinrich. *German Colonization Past and Future: The Truth About the German Colonies*. London: George Allen & Unwin, 1926.

Zimmerer, Jürgen. "The birth of the Ostland out of the spirit of colonialism: a postcolonial perspective on the Nazi policy of conquest and extermination." *Patterns of Prejudice* 39, no. 2 (2005): 197–219. http://search.ebscohost.com (22 September 2006).

Chapter Four:
Writing What We Teach

English and I

Masamitsu Murakami

> Masamitsu Murakami wrote this memoir at the same time as his Writing I students.

I TRY TO PRONOUNCE the v-sound. "Voo-Voo-Voo." It sounds weird. One of the reasons it sounds weird is that there is no v-sound in Japanese language. The other reason is that I try to pronounce the v-sound by putting the upper lip to the lower front teeth instead of putting the lower lip to the upper front teeth. "You looked like a bulldog back then," my mother often tells me when she talks about my childhood.

When I was three years old, my family lived in the Kochi prefecture, which is located in southwest Japan. I went to Minori Kindergarten, where English was taught as one of the electives. All I remember are the scenes where I was shown some cards. A drawing was printed on each card. When I was shown each card, I had to say what it was on the card in English. "It's a violin." "It's a tomato." "It's a dog." "It's a cat." Those scenes are now hidden within the shingled, wooden buildings of the kindergarten; however, it is certain that I encountered English in this kindergarten.

One day, when I came back from Osho Elementary school and was watching TV, Chu Arai, a famous comedian in Japan, said abruptly, "This is a pen." He often shouted this phrase out of context. It was a kind of gag. Now, I do not know what was so funny, but back then it was indeed funny and sensational. Almost all children in Japan would mimic him and repeat out of context, "This is a pen." Therefore, most of the children who loved Chu Arai memorized first in their lives "This is a pen." I was one of them. My English teacher was Chu Arai when I was an elementary school student.

In Japan, English education officially begins in junior high schools (though some students start to learn English in elementary schools). When I was a junior high school student, English education meant reading, writing, and grammar. Listening and speaking were never taught. The only sentence I remember from the textbook is "Canada is my country." Why did Canada appear in the textbook? I do not remember. I just recall Mr. Hamada, my English teacher in junior high school, loudly reading the textbook word by word in a Japanese accent while combing his remaining few strings of hair with his right hand.

High school English education in Japan further emphasizes reading, writing, and grammar. This is because students have to prepare for the entrance examinations of universities, which mainly test students' reading, writing, and grammatical knowledge. I do not remember what stories I read and who the teachers were. I just can visualize the teachers scribbling something on the blackboard. I cannot recall their faces. Their silhouettes are fused into the classrooms.

Thanks to these ghost teachers in high school, I was not admitted to any universities. Thus, I ended up going to the Sundai preparatory school, where the students were preparing for the next year's entrance examination. The lessons were of course designed to help students make it to universities; therefore, the English lessons emphasized reading, writing, and grammar. Instructors were just teaching tips to get good scores. Again, I cannot remember their names; I cannot recall their faces. Their figures dissipate into the blackboards.

After being refused by the universities again, I decided to go to the Sundai Foreign Language Institute, where I had American instructors for the first time in my life. At this foreign language institute, I also could learn listening and speaking in addition to reading, writing, and grammar.

One day, Kathy, my writing instructor, complimented me, saying, "You're very good at writing. Why don't you become a technical writer?" I do not know why Kathy recommended that I become a technical writer, but since then the words, "a technical writer," have never come apart from my brain. At that time however, I had no money to pursue a further academic endeavor; therefore, I had to work for a Japanese company for a while.

I worked for Uchimura Inc., which dealt with industrial rubber and resin. The problem was I was the only person who could understand English in that company. Therefore, in addition to the work I had to do as one of the sales representatives, I had to take care of all the documents written in English. Sometimes, the president asked me,

"Mr. Murakami, translate this document." Another time, my boss ordered me, "Murakami, translate this brochure." When our company expanded our business to the United States, I had to support one of our staff because he could not understand English at all. When our company established the Indonesian branch, I was in charge of supporting the Indonesian staff because English was the only way to communicate with them. As a result, there were always two towers of documents on my desk. Furthermore, I had to go out to do business with my customers. Before my heart stopped its move, I decided to leave the job. The good news was I had made enough money to study abroad.

Finishing the professional writing program at Missouri State University, I am now a graduate teaching assistant at MSU taking English 603. Dr. Baumlin is talking in front of me; my classmates are surrounding me. I speak, listen, read, and write in English. I am living with English. I try to pronounce the v-sound. I think it sounds perfect.

Finding My Team

Craig A. Meyer

> Craig A. Meyer contributed this memoir in conjunction with his Writing I classes.

I WAS ON A BASEBALL TEAM called the Bumblebees for several of my childhood years. We had bright yellow shirts with black letters and numbers. I loved those shirts. They gave me a sense of identity and belonging. I can remember how my teammates and I would win almost every game. The happy parents (of our team at least) always had a celebration. The party that followed was certain to have plenty of sugary fruit juices and various jiggling salads. These parties are where I learned to avoid "party" foods that had rainbow-like colors and shook more than the video *Rumpshaker*. As my support system, dad was at every game. Well—okay, not exactly a support system: he came mostly because the ball fields were across the street or he had to drive me to them.

I was never a star player, just the average outfielder who got a ball hit to him every two or three innings. There were times I would daydream about some alien race or commando group I had to attack to save everybody (and I do mean everybody: I was the last person who could do it). These "missions" were actually more fun than the baseball games. I can remember once or twice even running around the outfield acting out my Earth-saving story. In those times in which I was in never-never land and by some miracle a ball was hit to me, the yells from teammates and parents would snap me out of my daydream. I would dutifully retrieve the ball and throw it with my wimpy little arm as far as I could (which often was between shortstop and the pitcher on my best days). After I threw the ball back, I would feel bad for not paying better attention to the game, but that was soon replaced with an attack by Klingons that I had to defend against in order to save my home world.

After several years on the Bumblebees I was "traded," which is just a fancy term to say my parents didn't sign me up fast enough to be on the team that had been mine since I started playing baseball. The

Beetles was my new team, and I was about as excited about them then as I am now about my receding hairline. The first communication I had with the team's coach informed me that I needed to bring a white t-shirt to our first practice. *What? Are you telling me we don't have custom-printed color shirts?* Yep, no custom shirts, but plain white tees with the ever-colorful black marker to write "Beetles" at a forty-five degree angle across the chest. I suppose the angle was supposed to make it look cool, but it didn't. The writing on the shirt looked stupid—and cheap. After about twenty minutes of looking at this goofy shirt, I started to look at my new teammates. This team had some star players, which oddly were the coach's son and nephew, both named Mike. One of the Mikes was blond and the other had brown hair, which is how I ended up telling the two apart.

During one of our first games, I started running toward the outfield, but the coach called me back.

"You're playing catcher this game, OK?" he said.

I stared at him in confusion and then disgust. First, we did not have cool t-shirts, and second, I was told to be catcher. I considered my options. None. He guided me by the shoulders to the dreaded spot behind the plate, where baseballs come directly at your crotch at the speed of sound. As he guided me, he gave me basic directions for the position: catch the ball, throw it to the pitcher, and don't let any runner get by you—ever. That was it, no inspiring or profound statements about the position or parables to make me smile. Nothing.

There I am standing behind the plate with no protective gear, looking like an idiot with my plain white-and-black-magic-markered "Beetles" t-shirt and outfielder's glove. After several awkward moments of looking at my dad and at my old position in the outfield, the coach's wife ran over and dressed me in the proper gear: facemask (with helmet), chest plate (which covered my groin), and shin guards. She offered a consoling, "You'll do great!" as she trotted back to the stands. Great was the last thing on my mind.

Feeling like a little boy in a spacesuit, I knelt down and prepared to catch baseballs careening at my manhood. My mind began to wander through forests full of commandos waiting for me to eliminate them. Suddenly, a baseball walloped me in the chest plate, snapping me out of my daydream as I fell backward onto my butt. This obviously was not the place to fantasize about being Rambo. After several more throws, I began to get the hang of protecting my assets. While the baseball never got softer when I missed it, my skill compounded each week and I actually got better.

After each week's game there was no party, no celebration, and no nothing except a walk home with my dad. In the beginning, I missed the cheesy parties and dangerous food choices, but I learned that this team was different. They wanted to play baseball and go home. If I were to compare the two, my old team would be from the suburbs, and my new team would be from a trailer park. Both were good teams, just different.

Toward the end of the season with the Beetles, I actually liked the team that I once despised. We were winning games, and I was almost a star in my new position. The team depended on me each week to keep runs at bay, literally. Finally, it came down to one playoff game at Martin Luther King Jr. Park, the only game I ever played there. It was on the edge of the ghetto, but it was a clean and modernized park. This field was one of the best in the city, though my perspective of dirt never changed, so it did not matter to me. I remember that crowd being bigger than normal for our games, more family and friends. I know it was a playoff game but still it was the Beetles, not the Bumblebees. It seemed like every player had the whole family there—even my mom was there. My mom and sports is like a caveman and a computer. I was playing well, catching foul balls and striking fear into every runner who dared to round third—or at least that was my goal.

The game came down to the ninth inning and the mighty Beetles were up by one lonely run. The other team's first batter struck out after several futile swings. The next batter was their big boy—that is, he was over five foot six—as compared to the rest of us, barely five feet tall when standing on a soapbox. He swung his mighty bat and nailed the ball to centerfield. He rounded first but was halted there by our alert outfield (now that I was not out there). The next batter was a smaller boy with an Ichabod Crane-type walk who had just about as much grace when swinging at nothing but air. He swung well before the ball was even near the plate, which made me laugh out loud. Finally, after two strikes he hit the ball in a unique way: he swung at the ball, missed and as he was spinning around the second time, he hit the ball! He didn't even know he had hit it when I jumped up and snatched the ball, tagging him out. Even his coach was laughing at him. The next batter arrived at the plate and had the gall to say, "Watch this."

This newest batter was about my size and build with a Louisville Slugger in his hands. Every player knows that a Slugger is the bat of champions. He tapped his cleats with the mystical bat, then readied his body to smack one beyond the fence. The first pitch he let go: it was a little outside and low. I could tell this was no ordinary moment; the crowd had hushed, and I could feel tension in the air. I cautiously tossed it back to the pitcher. The second pitch was right on the money, but he didn't bite on that one either. As I was kneeling back down after throwing the ball back, he deepened the trench beneath his right foot with his cleats, kicking dirt on my plate. GAME ON. Nobody but *nobody* kicks dirt on my plate; I shot back up ready to confront the transgressor. The umpire yelped "Time!" and showed his backside to my teammates as he swept off the plate. Order was restored.

I knelt back down and got ready to receive fastballs and curveballs. As the next pitch came, I saw the Louisville Slugger draw back and begin to swing. The bat hit the ball with a crushing blow that sent it to my old homeland of left field. The runner on first took off like a rocket. The outfield was just getting a handhold on the ball as the runner whipped around second base. The third base coach was yelling, "GO, GO, GO!" to big boy as he neared third. The outfielder heaved the baseball toward me with everything he had. The ball bounced once and I caught it—solid. With ball in mitt, I threw off my helmet and facemask. The runner had just rounded third, and his coach in the dugout screamed, "Bowl him over! Bowl him over!" I clenched my teeth.

I planted myself in front of my plate to defend it. As I tightened my grip on the ball, I could feel the stitches through the leather of my outfield glove. I looked into his eyes and he into mine, we both had an uncertainty: who was going to win? Big boy's mouth was open and sucking in air. The crowd was still crying out, but I did not listen to them anymore. I widened my stance to cover more ground and lowered my left shoulder, ready to receive whatever he had to offer. I took a deep breath and held it. As I waited, I could hear every crunch of his feet on the dirt mixed with the tightened pounding of my heart deep in my chest. Below my armpit, sweat ran down, tempting me to laugh by its tickling gesture. I would have none of it. His arms rose as he began to dive headfirst into me like a linebacker in football. Big boy plowed into me like a tsunami hitting the beach. I could only hope that I held firm. His blow sent me off to the side onto my right elbow; we went down side by side, lying face to face on the fine gravel ground. Dust covered my tongue and clouded my vision. I felt dizzy.

I did not know if I had stopped the run or not. My adversary jumped up and began to walk off to his dugout, as if nothing had happened. His face was expressionless, as if he scored the run but did not want to rub it in my face. A look of despair crossed my face as I realized I may not have stopped him. After several confused seconds, I rolled over to look at the umpire, and he yelled with all he had, "OUT!" The crowd celebrated.

I slowly rose to the cheers of my teammates and coach. My elbow hurt and was bleeding. Our coach was still applauding my effort as he helped me to my feet. He yanked me into his armpit for a half-hug as I said, "I hurt my elbow, Coach."

"You'll be fine. You stopped him cold. Good job!"

My team surrounded me, slapped me on the back, and screamed in pure joy. I could hear my mom in the background whooping it up. Clearly, she was insane. For the first time, there was an after-game party. I'm sure it was in my honor. The celebration was not like the ones with the Bumblebees, where rainbow drinks and wiggling salads ruled. We, the trailer park team, went to McDonald's. At that moment, there was nothing better than a cheeseburger, fries, and *my* team.

Modestly Speaking: Wendy Shalit's "The Future of Modesty"

Meg Johnson

> Meg Johnson wrote this textual analysis at the same time as her Writing I students.

WENDY SHALIT DESCRIBES in her essay "The Future of Modesty" the beginning of a revolution. Modesty, in her opinion, is making a fashionable return to a society that idealizes sexuality and bare women. In "The Future of Modesty," Shalit states many key themes and ideas. Some of what she explores are the changes from an immodest culture to one that is slowly embracing modesty, how our sexualized culture has permeated our own ideas of modesty, and finally, the numbing of women to their own femininity and sexuality. Today we cannot escape the images of women all over television and in magazines. However, are we really like these women? As women, do we enjoy being paraded around bare breasted and scantily clad for all to see? Shalit examines why she believes we are returning to a culture of modesty from immodest beginnings.

Wendy Shalit is an Orthodox Jewish woman who controversially protested unisex bathrooms at her alma mater, Williams College. She began the revolution with her first book, *A Return to Modesty*, and in the essay "The Future of Modesty," Shalit describes a culture of modern women who are "learning their social graces," and "changing their fundamental attitude about sex" (254). The immodesty of our foremothers has become so extreme, Shalit argues, that we cannot become any more immodest. Therefore, we are left with only one alternative—modesty. Shalit explains that we had once conformed to immodesty because it was in fashion. She cites a personal example from the response to her article against the coed bathrooms: "It became clear to me that in fact many college students were like me, uncomfortable with not having privacy, but not wanting to seem 'uncool' by objection" (253). However, the conformity that Shalit describes has not quite disappeared from women today. In many cases, in fact, being cool is still a big priority. For example, women and men still favor cohabitation over marriage. Also, more often than not, both sexes openly live with each other in communal housing (much like dormitories but off the college campuses). This behavior often involves showering and brushing together in the same bathroom, yet it is becoming modestly acceptable.

The overabundance of sexuality on television and in magazines has permeated our culture: "sex sells" is a common marketplace philosophy. For example, this October's issue of *Cosmopolitan*—the alleged "Bible for Women"—has some eye-catching articles: "30 Sex Boosters," "Discover the Sex Fantasy 80% of Men Have," and let us not forget Christina Aguilera's breasts. Contrary to the *Cosmo* cover, Shalit proclaims that "women are changing their fundamental attitude about sex" (254) and polls *Glamour* to validate her point.

Similarly, the alleged "Lusty Lady" of New York's liberal online news source *The Village Voice*—otherwise known as Rachel Kramer Bussel—has her own interesting perspective on the matter of modesty. A self-proclaimed sex goddess, she parades around the Big Apple in midnight sexual escapades and then writes about her encounters in her weekly column. Recently, however, this bawdy gal has had a change of heart and embarked on her very own sexual hiatus. Bussel writes in her article "Coochie on Lock":

> I recently disabused a friend from the notion that being a sex columnist makes for dating nirvana. In fact, nothing could be further form the truth; we may get propositioned, but those who think we're sex goddesses who can fulfill their every fantasy are dead wrong, and only see a fraction of the bigger picture. Sex columnist or not, it's actually tough to figure out . . . who wants to know the real me. . . . (Bussel)

She goes on to write, "Deciding to take a break is selfish on one level: it forces me to deal with what I like and don't like about myself. . . . Choosing to be content on my own, instead of rushing online or to the nearest bar or party to find 'the one,' has given me space to focus on me." Bussel has declared that yes, the "sexual goddess" herself is looking for something a little deeper. Shalit believes that it is precisely this attitude that has marked one of the most momentous turns from immodesty to modesty. She writes that "immodesty isn't, finally, as sexy as we thought it was going to be" (255).

This change of focus is very important: all of a sudden our sexual climate has changed from very heated and casual to something with meaning. Shalit notices this trend and claims it is calling us back to modesty. If women are prowling the city for sexual encounters, their dress and attitude reflect the immodesty of the past. Today, however, women are putting casual sex on the back burner, telling men "no" more often than not. Baring breasts and legs would make their "no" sound weak rather than resounding like they want.

Shalit describes society on the whole as sexually numb. She writes that if "prevailing wisdom decrees 'hook ups' don't matter, that sex is 'no big deal,' then we must numb ourselves in order to go through with it" (256). This statement deals with her earlier remarks about not wanting to be seen as "uncool," or going along with the majority vote for the sake of conformity. Shalit knows women are seeing the change in the sexual climate as good and healthy as well as fruitful. Nothing unwholesome will come of women holding out for a good man. Not only will they be able to experience a happy and healthy sex life, they also have a good relationship as well.

Shalit worries that women might be going along with the immodest flow just to do it. She prescribes a cure for immodesty, stating that "we just need to stop drinking so much, get off our Prozac, and come out of the closet about it" (256). Interestingly, Shalit does not prescribe celibacy or prudishness as one might expect from her religious ancestors. Instead, she is just warning against doing something for all the wrong reasons. She cautions women who have not seen the modest trend to wake up and smell the coffee. Today it is not just about sex finally: it is about something more than that. Shalit herself is waiting "for something more exciting" (256). She writes: "I don't want to settle for less and . . . I don't think you should have to, either" (256).

Shalit and Bussel see that instead of focusing on the internal, women are drowning their low self-esteem, sorrow, and pain in casual sex, a temporary solution. Bussel's "choosing to be content on my own" is a powerful phrase. "On my own," should be the mantra for modest women everywhere. Not only is today's modern woman embracing her own sexuality, she is independent: her own self. Shalit concludes her essay by asking, "What would happen if [women] stopped listening to those who say womanhood is a drug, and began to see themselves as individuals with the power to turn society around?" (257). She answers, "Society might very well have to turn around" (257).

Women can find freedom in solidarity without celibacy. We do not have to be prudish in order to avoid promiscuousness. Women only need to be confident. Finally, in order to relieve ourselves of our zombie states, all we need is a good dose of reality. In order for a woman to be confident and beautiful, she does not have to bare all. In fact, Shalit believes that modest women are more alluring than scantily clad ones. There is something beautiful to celebrate in our imperfections and curves. Modestly, we are the strongest definition of beautiful.

Works Cited

Bussel, Rachel Kramer. "Coochie on Lock." *The Village Voice*. 7
Sept. 2006. 15 Sept. 2006.
<http://villagevoice.com/people/0637,bussel,74402,24.html>.

Shalit, Wendy. "The Future of Modesty." *The Presence of Others:
Voices and Images that Call for Response*. Ed. Lunsford and
Ruszkiewicz. Boston: Bedford/St. Martins, 2004. 251–257.

A Graduate Assistant's Observations of Popular Culture in the Classroom

Jessica Glover

Jessica Glover wrote this I-Search at the same time as her Writing I students.

Beavis: This video's got, like, words and stuff in it.
Butt-head: Words suck. If I wanted to read, I'd go to college.
Mike Judge, Beavis and Butt-head

THE IMPORTANT ROLE POPULAR culture plays within today's classrooms was not made relevant to me until I asked the students in my freshman English class to "free write" for fifteen minutes about the events of their weekend. Most students wrote about their experiences with college life: being homesick, missing their girlfriend or boyfriend, or trying to get caught up on homework. However, one student's response came as a complete shock to me. Honestly, to some degree, I was left feeling disappointed with today's youth. The student took two entire pages to describe how he had been in a terrible mood the previous week because he had not had time to play his Xbox. He wrote how he had been excited about the weekend since he planned on devoting all of his time to his gaming. Come Monday morning, the student was very upset because he had spent his entire weekend trying to reach a certain level and was unable to defeat the game. The student continued describing how he had put off all his homework and refused to consult the game's guidebook because that would mean he was personally admitting defeat.

Ordinarily, this would not be an entry that would stand out to readers and especially not one that would shock a reader. In fact, I know several fellow students who pass through college giving minimal attention to their studies. However, I was amazed not with the student's lack of concern for his grade but with the assumptions concerning teaching I had made prior to this school year. Upon personal reflection, I now realize that I had expected all of my students to approach the class with the same level of excitement that I have for English. I wanted to mold and have my students devour

|113|

literature, perhaps even changing the way they view the world. Now, almost halfway through the semester, I was faced with the harsh realization that many students were, in fact, gaming their weekends away and writing their papers the day before the assignment was due.

I was reading a journal from a healthy male in his early twenties who had the opportunity to go to college in America (arguably the most prosperous society in the history of humankind), and his entire weekend was ruined because he could not reach the next level on his Xbox. After this event, I decided I needed to understand further what it means to teach the Gaming Generation.

I understood that I was approaching teaching with expectations I had gathered from mass media as well. I had envisioned a classroom as portrayed in *To Sir with Love*, *Mr. Holland's Opus*, *Dead Poet's Society*, and at worst *Dangerous Minds*. The common thread between all of Hollywood's portrayals of first-year teachers is that the teacher eventually triumphs and wins over the students in the classroom, changing their lives forever. I never expected the harsh reality that the majority of students pass through a class barely remembering their teacher's name. Hollywood had left me unprepared. I had to look elsewhere for understanding.

In the book *Everything Bad Is Good For You*, Steven Johnson states, "You have to shed your expectations about older cultural forms to make sense of the new. Game players are not soaking up moral counsel, life lessons, or rich psychological portraits. They are not having emotional experiences with their Xbox, other than the occasional adrenaline rush" (39). It is this instant adrenaline rush that causes gaming to become addictive. According to Professor Mark Griffins, "They are the types of games that completely engross the player. They are not games that you can play for twenty minutes and stop" ("S. Korean Dies after Games Session"). Obviously, creators of such video games want players to be challenged, spending countless hours immersed in their character's world. Consumers will pay larger amounts of money for games that take weeks, months, and even years to play. In games such as *World of Warcraft*, players develop their characters in a virtual world alongside other gamers via the Internet. The longer one plays, the more advanced the character becomes. Players can acquire housing, jobs, and unlimited material possessions for their character. Their character's physical appearance can be shaped at will in such a manner as to attract other characters, opening limitless guilt-free options for the player to experience. Players are able to virtually play out their fantasy life without the pressures and constraints of human interaction and regulations. Even the law of gravity is not relevant, leaving players with superhuman abilities, if they have the time to advance their character through hours of gaming. For these reasons, some gamers find the virtual world in which they develop their character much more appealing than their actual daily life. At this point, one must ask the question: when does virtual reality simply become reality?

Even keeping this in mind, the idea of classifying gamers as addicts still seemed a somewhat extreme assessment, until I continued my research. According to Sabine Grüsser from the Interdisciplinary Addiction Research Group of the Charité hospital, "Excessive playing of computer games presumably activates the same structures in the brain as drugs do" ("Study: Computer Games Can Lead to Addiction"). Grüsser says that addictions stem from relying too heavily on one coping strategy, which eventually becomes the only activity that can activate the dopamine system and bring a person relief. "It's the same mechanism in all addicts," Grüsser says ("Study: Computer Games Can Lead to Addiction"). As with any addiction, without moderation the effect can be devastating to the individual and other persons in his or her life. Maressa Hecht Orzack, who founded a computer addiction service at McLean Hospital in Boston, agrees that the condition has a lot in common with other addictions (Motluk). What makes video game addiction more complex is that gamers cannot simply abstain from using computers—they are now an integral part of our lives (Motluk). Even within my own class, I require all homework assignments and papers to be typed before handing them in, and the majority of research can be conducted by use of the Internet. For that reason, Orzack suggests the addition has to be approached in the same way as an eating disorder (Motluk).

I was still skeptical as to whether this addiction was only seen in gaming fanatics or whether it was possible that a percentage of my own students would be classified as addicts to video gaming. If this was the case, how is teaching the gaming generation different from previous generations of college students? I quickly learned that I was not the first to ask these types of questions. The results of a recent health survey at Michigan State University concluded that 18.5% of their students reported that spending time online and playing computer games had caused them to get a lower grade on a test, a lower grade in a class or to drop a class altogether (Munn). When this was compared with drinking, only 8.5% stated that drinking had the same effect (Munn). When the study was separated by sex, 13% of women reported the Internet or gaming had negative effects on their schoolwork; for men it was a hefty 25.2% (Munn). Suddenly, the shock over one student's journal entry paled in comparison to the results. There was no longer a question as to whether or not I would be teaching video gamers, but rather, how to reach such students while teaching them.

Teaching gamers requires an increased level of motivation to gain the attention of the student. In order to be an effective teacher, I would need to become familiar with other teachers' pedagogies. An effective pedagogical intervention, according to Sholte and Denski, "must allow students to speak from their own experiences at the same time that it encourages them to identify and unravel the codes of popular culture that may work to . . . silence and disempower them" (Alvermann 140).

First, one must embrace the fact that today's American society is saturated with mass media. The book *Popular Culture in the Classroom* by Donna Alvermann mentions the fact that "[w]e are living in an age often portrayed as being dominated by consumer capitalism and the products of a capitalism culture—for example, shopping malls, newspapers, talk shows, Music Television (MTV) and the World Wide Web" (2). There is no way to live in today's American society and remain completely blocked from the influence of mass media that the general public is bombarded with daily. Often this influence starts at such a young age that the general public does not realize how much of an impact popular culture plays in determining their individuality. Michael Berube, in his essay "The 'Elvis Costello Problem' in Teaching Popular Culture," theorizes that "the advent of 'classic' pop culture means, among other things, that the cultural dreck of your childhood has somehow survived to become the cultural dreck of your children's childhood" (5).

The influence of popular culture on the general public can also have an effect on the literacy of a nation. As *Popular Culture and Critical*

Pedagogy: Reading, Constructing, Connecting reports, "From the moment that Big Bird introduces them as children to the letter *a* on *Sesame Street*, students begin developing a literacy about popular culture that may be deepened and refined in a composition course so that they can perceive the way that representation shapes culture and influences their lives" (Daspit 35). Even with this direct correlation to popular culture, some individuals still feel that teaching popular culture within the college setting is not appropriate or lacks educational value. According to the book *Teaching Popular Culture: Beyond Radical Pedagogy* by David Buckingham, "The hyperbolic rhetoric of 'critical pedagogy' has come under attack not only from theoretical perspectives such as feminism, anti-racism, and postmodernism, but also in light of actual classroom experience. The notion that teachers might 'liberate' students through rationalistic forms of ideological critique has been increasingly questioned, not only on the grounds of its political arrogance, but also because of its ineffectiveness in practice" (23). Thus, I would have to decide whether or not I would use popular culture as a teaching tool within my college classes.

After reading further, I began to realize the immense affect mass media has on everyone, myself included. I wanted to know whether or not my students were aware of the influence mass media has in their lives as well. Once I decided I would be researching the use of popular culture in the classroom, I wanted to conduct a small case study using my English 110 and English 203 students. Since these are two different types of classes, one a structured composition class and the other a creative writing class, I hypothesized that I would experience very different reactions about popular culture from each. I kept in mind the points made in the book *Miss Grundy Doesn't Teach Here Anymore* edited by Diane Penrod: "Students should be encouraged to analyze common objects as representations of dynamic culture, using critical methodologies like rhetoric, ethnography, and semiotics to question the kinds of knowledge present in their worlds" (1). As a teacher, I face the difficult task of presenting icons that have become so ordinary and accepted as strange and unique to our culture. In order to achieve this goal, one must know how to open up a perspective "outside" of popular culture from which to view the icons.

In my English 110 class, I wrote the following quote from Charles Paine's *The Resistant Writer* on the board, "Students come to the classrooms with models of argument and selfhood that are derived from the mass media" (159). I also added a quote from Lynn Z. Bloom, "Like swimmers passing through the chlorine bath, students must first be disinfected in freshman English" (qtd. in Paine 158). I asked the students to take ten minutes to respond. They were further instructed to take a few minutes to think about each quote before coming to their answer, but not to contemplate the quote too long because I wanted their initial reaction as well. After having read *The Resistant Writer*, I knew that "student writers strive to understand 'who they are' and 'who they might become' *through* their investigations of culture and the ideas of others; and they strive to understand their culture and the ideas of others *through* their investigations of themselves" (18). I was hoping this assignment would not only be beneficial to my personal research on popular culture, but that it would also allow students to reflect on conclusions that some scholars have documented about the Generation X student.

Later in the week, I collected their journals and eagerly read their responses. Within the responses, ten out of twenty-one journals collected were instantly offended by the quotes and disagreed with the assumption made about them. As I had assumed, approximately half of the class was not aware of the influence mass media has in their lives. Those ten students argued that they were not influenced at all by mass media because their family, friends, peers, and religions influenced them. One student was completely shocked by the notion that scholars were studying Generation X students like they were "lab rats." More astounding to me was the fact that five of the ten students wrote entries to the effect that they did not care what anyone thought of them. One student responded, "No one is going to listen to what I have to say, so why should I care what they say about freshmen." Another student stated that she[1] did not feel her opinion on the matter was going to change anything, so she did not see why she needed to respond at all. These types of responses only supported what is being said about Generation X students.

---

[1] The author did not wish to reveal the gender of her students. To avoid the awkward "s/he" and "his/her" constructions or the non-standard "they" and "their," the editors (who know nothing about the students specified) have chosen to arbitrarily render this student as "she," the student in the following paragraph as "he," and the student in the next to the last paragraph again as "she."

The other eleven students agreed with the quotes. Some commented about Bloom and how they had already learned more in their English class in half a semester in college than in all four years in high school. One student further commented that students do need to be "disinfected" to prepare them for the expectations of college professors. Others responded that they were trying to break from the influence of mass media by going to college. Perhaps my favorite response of all was from a student who commented that he[2] was initially insulted by the quotes on the board, but once he reflected for a moment on the quotes, he could honestly admit that he had to agree with Paine and Bloom. The student went on to say that he knew that I had intentionally put those quotes on the board to get a reaction from students so they would critically think about how the world is viewing them as the next generation of learners: he, however, was not going to give me the satisfaction of hearing his response. (Ah-ha, one might be on to me.) I am always amazed by the diverse personalities teachers encounter within the classroom.

I applied Laura Gray-Rosendale's reflections on the situation of a student who does not merely respond to the rhetorical situation as it is constructed by the question but moves beyond it. What if students do not cooperate with the rather fixed constraints of the question, but instead uses their "power of response" to interpret the question's meaning? Gray-Rosendale states, "The student must first recognize the myriad tensions at work within the situation itself, and then carefully think through how to utilize her or his power of response in the most effective and convincing ways possible" (qtd. in Penrod 151). I was glad to see a few of the students challenging and questioning the quotes from scholars on the board. I followed up class discussion with Paine's notion that "At the heart of critical thinking lies the ability to distance oneself from one's world, to step back and critically think about thinking, one's own thinking and one's community thinking" (157). I then started the class discussion over their critical analysis papers.

In the English 203 class, I began class discussion with a brief preface on how a poet must have a keen eye, much like a photographer or any other artist: poets must view their world in a unique way and be able to relay what they see to the world through their writing. I then

---

[2] See previous footnote.

focused their sight to "Pop Culture," which I wrote in bold letters on the board. As Michael Berube mentions in his essay "The 'Elvis Costello Problem' in Teaching Popular Culture": "Most of the outcry against teaching popular culture in college courses takes this form: The subject, we are told, is unworthy of serious study, lacking the textual and cultural density that defines the masterworks of the arts and humanities" (1). Keeping this in mind, I instructed the students to write for ten minutes about the affects of popular culture on our society, what images jumped into their heads, and how they could play on these pop cultural icons within their poetry. I wanted to teach them to think critically about the present by making it debts to, and differences from, the distant cultural past. I also knew I would receive a wide variety of subject matter, because as Michael Berube mentions, "The problem with teaching popular culture is: while so much of it is transitory and ephemeral, so much of it, surprisingly enough, seems to be here to stay" (5). The term "popular culture" is difficult to delimit in subject matter or put into a timeframe.

Before I was able to open class discussion, all of the students began talking amongst themselves about what particular pop culture reference came to mind. Students who normally shy away from class discussion were laughing and openly discussing their opinions. I decided to remain quiet for a few minutes as the class exploded into conversation, their discussions overlapping as they flung comments across the room. The students connected to the subject so well that I had to stand on my chair to get their attentions again.

Using popular culture references to engage students in active class discussion worked very well, almost too well. I found that when introducing popular culture in any class, teachers must focus class discussion and not leave the forum completely open. It is important also to limit how much class time is spent discussing popular culture. Focusing too much on popular culture can cause fear, either a fear that students cannot handle more traditional topics or that we as teachers cannot.

In the following weeks I noticed several students turned in poems using popular cultural metaphors and even some poems completely dedicated to popular icons and subjects. When the time arrived to workshop such pop-culturally centered poems, I was eager to introduce them to similar works, such as Frank O'Hara's "The Day

Lady Died" and Ai's dramatic monologue from Marilyn Monroe's perspective. Perhaps my favorite poem from a student was a brief haiku: "God created man / Man killed God and now / Women will rule the world." The student declared that she[3] was inspired by the box office hit *Jurassic Park*. Will this student have a future profession in poetry? Probably not, however, I was delighted to see that she was beginning to actively engage in the class's critiques and was putting forethought into her poetry. While many teachers still feel using popular culture is a way to "dumb down" a lesson, I was able to use popular culture as a "stepping stone" or necessary bridge to allow students to learn to think and function in both the common and academic realms.

With the use of daily journal writing, I have tried to instill the importance student responses can have in the classroom. It was helpful for me to keep in mind W.F. Garrett-Petts' comment that, "Present-day audiences will be tomorrow's authors of relatively complex image/text productions—and understanding the rhetoric of this new electronically mediated or otherwise 'hybridized' vernacular should be of concern to those of us who teach both literature and literacies" (qtd. Penrod 78). Laura Gray-Rosendale also emphasizes its importance when she suggests that "[t]o encourage students to fully acknowledge their power of response identity construction and audience development in the face of any assignment given is to encourage them to become skillful rhetorical thinkers"(qtd. in Penrod 157). By gradually incorporating pop culture into the classroom every day and by pushing students to think critically about the world in which they live, I hope that such teaching will have relevancy in the students' personal lives outside the classroom, creating well-rounded, critical thinkers who value themselves and the purpose they serve in the world.

---

[3] See footnote 1.

Works Cited

Alvermann, Donna E., Jennifer S. Moon, and Margaret C. Hagood. *Popular Culture in the Classroom: Teaching and Researching Critical Media Literacy*. Illinois: International Reading Association and the National Reading Conference, 1999.

Berube, Michael. "The 'Elvis Costello Problem' in Teaching Popular Culture." *Chronicle of Higher Education*. 13 Aug. 1999. B4+.

Buckingham, David. *Teaching Popular Culture: Beyond Radical Pedagogy*. New York: University of New York Press, 1998.

Daspit, Toby, and John A. Weaver, eds. *Popular Culture and Critical Pedagogy: Reading, Constructing, Connecting*. New York: Garland Publishing, 2000.

Johnson, Steven. *Everything Bad is Good For You: How Today's Popular Culture Is Actually Making Us Smarter*. New York: Riverhead Books, 2005.

Motluk, Alison. "Gaming Fanatics Show Signs of Drug Addiction." *New Scientist.com*. 16 Nov. 2005. *Free Republic*. 1 June 2007 <http://www.freerepublic.com/focus/f-news/1524570/posts>.

Munn, James. "Gaming Addiction Worse than Alcohol?" *Aeropause*. 22 September 2006 <http://www.aeropause.com/archives/2006/09/internet_gaming.php>.

Paine, Charles. *The Resistant Writer: Rhetoric as Immunity, 1850 to the Present*. New York: State University of New York Press, 1999.

Penrod, Diane, ed. *Miss Grundy Doesn't Teach Here Anymore: Popular Culture and the Composition Classroom*. New Hampshire: Boynton/Cook Publishers, 1997.

"S. Korean Dies after Games Session." *BBC News Front Page*. 10 Aug. 2005. *BBC News*. 01 June 2007 <http://news.bbc.co.uk/2/hi/technology/4137782.stm>.

"Study: Computer Games Can Lead to Addiction." *DW-World. Deutsche Welle*. 2005. *Deutsche Welle*. 01 June 2007 <http://www.dw-world.de/dw/article/0,2144,1773386,00.html>.

Just Being Practical

Lanette Cadle

> Lanette Cadle wrote this essay at the same time as her Writing II
> students in response to the Persuasive Narrative assignment.

THERE I WAS IN MY CAMEL broadcloth jacket, professionally-tousled
hair, and contact lenses, joining the crowd of my peers. They were a
nice looking bunch. Friendly, tanned to an appropriate turn for the
season, necktied or blazered, and ready, really ready to learn. The
motivational speaker was one of a happy stream of shiny faces I'd
listened to. This one was thirty-fiveish, polished, but wise, oh, wise in
the ways of salesmanship in ways I would never be. It was at the
Kansas State Realtor's® quarterly meeting, and he was making a
point.

"Spell Albuquerque," he said. I did it. He smiled, a flicker at one
corner only. This was the payoff. "Now spell it backward." The point,
I think, was something about brains only taking you so far, or that
there are some things no one can do. I'll never know now, because I
wrecked the whole setup by spelling Albuquerque backward—
without hesitation. The whole presentation skittered a bit at that
point, but he was a pro and saved it by asking me how I did that,
made sure no one else wanted to try (bubbling laughter from the
crowd), and continued on with his spiel. I felt foreign.

Here's how it was done. It's simple. When I spell, I see the word
clearly, much like 12-point Courier New on good, heavy-rag paper. I
then just read it off. Since the word is fully visualized, reading
backwards takes a fraction of a second more time, but no more effort.
This method has great benefits for classes like Art History as well. All
those slides and notes are there, in that pin-point visualization spot
between the eyes and one inch up, packed up, stored, and ready to
view—at least for short-term memory. Just like for anyone else, using
this method for long-term memory takes more effort and upkeep, but
for snippets like spelling words, it's unbeatable. Mr. Motivation made
sure everyone there knew how it was done and how incredibly
uncommon it is. He moved past whatever his point was and switched

to deal-breaking verbal strategies, how to recognize them, and how to beat them. Back in my seat, I pretended to take notes.

I USED TO READ THE DICTIONARY for fun when I was in elementary school and never told anyone about it, knowing even then that most people would much rather spend their spare time rustling up a dodge ball game or playing cops and robbers on bikes. So would I, at least the nine-year-old me, but I also had to *know*, and the dictionary was the entrance-exam to another world, one I didn't know yet, but one I didn't intend to be excluded from. In the meantime, I read and edited my father's work memos and took typing in summer school.

BEING A REALTOR® IS A good job for a woman who needs to make money, real money. When I began, it was a good way to add a few extra thousand a year to my husband's upwardly-mobile income for vacations and frivols. Later, it was a ready method for real money for a single mom of two. Small town America tends to place people in a limited number of categories, and there's only so much room for each one: a few ministers, some lawyers, a sprinkling of small business owners, and a vast morass of consumers in pickup trucks and tank tops on their way to Wal-Mart. One of the best lessons in listing I ever got was from my first broker, Ruth. When we were short of listings she would push herself back from her desk and say, "We're almost out of paper towels," and wink. We'd go to Wal-Mart and somewhere between the cronies at the snack bar, the housewives checking perfume before school lets out, and the cashiers, she'd get one, sometimes two, appointments with someone who wanted to sell their house. They just didn't know it before she needed paper towels.

For really fast and easy money—and that first year as a single mom I needed it badly—Ruth advised selling mobile homes. In Kansas, mobile homes count as personal property in the same way as vehicles rather than as real property. As long as they aren't on a permanent foundation, the commission is high and the paperwork is low. Even better, the turnaround is lightning fast with a high possibility of a cash sale. Later, when I was a managing broker for another firm, one of the top producers at another branch told me in vivid detail during a car trip to yet another motivational speaker session how easy it is to make money selling cars. He admitted the hours were even worse than real estate (I was working 60–80 hours a week at that point, as were many of my good agents), but spun out a series of nostalgic tales about gullible customers and little to no regulation that shocked what was left of my sales innocence. Easy money, he crooned, and most in the car agreed and chimed in on the mantra.

However, the need to live aside, I still had limits. Selling mobiles was as far as I was willing to go. In the reckless abandon that was the byproduct of buying frenzy, most mobile buyers waived mechanical inspections, trusting their own handyman sense and feeling an aversion to paying anyone to do anything that they could conceivably do themselves. Sometimes this led to nasty phone calls the morning after the first cold snap when the furnace didn't work, but for the most part I felt no guilt. Even without a furnace, those mobiles were their first step toward homeownership and away from an ever more squalid rental life. I felt saintly as I gave them the phone number for a local heating and air firm.

All the same, there were times that I wondered about the, for lack of a better word, "rightness" of what I was doing. Once for a closing gift I gave a giant rubber cockroach to stick on the buyer's refrigerator, in memory of the rental house they left behind; it was so roach-infested that the bugs found a way into their refrigerator and danced on the food inside, most likely waggling their little antennae in glee. In order to pass the time while he read the contract, I counted the husband's tattoos, moving up from the roman numerals on his knuckles to the tiny tear drops at the corner of his left eye. When he looked down to read I saw an open eye tattooed on each lid. His wife watched him read, her waist-length hair streaked with gray and her face creased with deep lines. She was twenty-eight.

IN HIGH SCHOOL I TOOK creative writing for the easy A and found that it was easy, but also found that stopping was not. I wrote the filler poems for the literary journal, the ones that never showed up in submissions, but were needed to make the right rhythm for the reader: poem, poem, poem, drawing, story, poem. I found an old journal a few days ago with a poem fragment in it. The poet at fifteen.

JANUARIES ARE SLOW, AND SOMEONE has to man the phones. I started writing again. Nothing serious, just a little mystery novel to pass the time. It made me look busy when clients came in, which was all for the good. I stopped when I realized that the small moments inside the plot interested me far more than the plot itself. Writing poetry never occurred to me, not even for a moment. I knew no one who read poetry and made the connection that no readers equals no royalty advance. You see, I thought I was going to get paid for writing.

Later, post-real estate and after I returned to school, my advisor said, take ESL, you'll always be in demand. I took Intro to Creative Writing for that slot on the English Education degree plan anyway. There wasn't room for any more, though, and my advisor looked down his glasses at me and warned that I would be best served by something more practical.

It was the most practical class I ever took. Sure, the syllabus scared me at first. Carrying the books to my car, I muttered over and over in different rhythms, "Nine poems and two stories. NINE poem and two stories. Nine POEMS and two stories." I never doubted my ability to write the stories, but the poems, the poems. Poetry was alien, a land dreamed of but never inhabited. I wrote the first one, then the next. I said to my instructor, also the coordinator for the MFA program, that I wanted to make money writing and doubted that poetry could do that. He laughed so hard he started wheezing, then he stopped and said, "My God, you're serious," and explained the realities of this writing life. He wouldn't tell me which genre was my strongest, but suggested that I take one more course in each the next semester to find out. There was a course conflict between Nature of Poetry (required) and Fiction Workshop, so Poetry Workshop was the winner. I got it approved by getting a brand-new advisor to sign off on my schedule while my regular one was at a conference. Some negotiations work best using sleight of hand.

IT WOULD SOUND MORE NOBLE and fitting if I inserted an epiphany here about how I made the switch to writing. You know—how the heavens part and I slap my forehead hard, shouting "Oy! I should be writing! Enough of this tacky sales life." However, in real life I got canned.

I was managing broker of an office that was yet to make money. My predecessor was a veteran broker, but in her seventies with a penchant for nabbing sales instead of passing them on to agents. There was office unrest, and I was the solution. Unfortunately after four months of trying to recruit more agents and having my efforts shot down by the existing agents who saw the potential influx of seasoned, heavy-hitter agents as less business for them, I was out too. I was replaced by a man I had been dating; apparently our breakup was a career move. I held no grudge though, and wished him the best. Offers from four other companies came in within twenty-four hours, but I questioned whether diving back in was the right thing to do. I fell back on savings and child support.

Later, when I was through with my B.A. and working on an MFA in Poetry out-of-state, I heard that he didn't last either. The company owner took over as manager and, surprise, also didn't make the office turn around. My theory that it was a toxic office in a bad location proved true, and the unfortunate result was his bankruptcy and losing all of his offices to an out-of-town competitor. They immediately closed my former branch. This shouldn't cheer me—but it does.

MY DAUGHTER IS MAKING the rounds of colleges and thinking about majors and what they may or may not lead to. She's picked her school and the housing contract is sent along with a whopping check, so that's settled. The major is a sore spot, though. She's a good writer, a better one than I'll admit to her face. All the same, her first choice for a major was elementary education, despite the fact that she really doesn't like children that much. It was practical, it led to a capital-J job in the end, and that was a big concern for her. I don't know what to say. What kind of credibility do I have at this point? I chased dollars with the best of them and put in the hours. She has childhood memories of being my "personal assistant" and coloring at the conference table while I closed a deal. She knows it was just a job and I did it anyway, just like most of the parents of her friends in that small town.

Just being practical sounds good, but needs to be carefully defined. I didn't really face up to my own best self until I realized that money meant little to me compared to the freedom to write and to learn, not only for a few years in school, but for a lifetime. Her best self may be something else, but I pray that she goes for it and ignores the whispers about what is practical and what is not.

I was reading her portfolio at semester's end and marveled at the strong voice and sharp images. Against all odds, she is a poet. She talks about choices, what careers leave time for writing. She also thinks about genres, mourning that poetry pays so little when it pays at all. I say, "So you think someone's going to pay you to write?" This time we both start laughing—gut-busting, belly-splitting laughter that won't quit until the tears spill down my cheeks, the kind of laughter that hurts where it doesn't show.

Welcome to South Dakota

Jane Hoogestraat

> Jane Hoogetraat wrote this personal essay at the same time as her Writing II: Writing for Graduate and Professional Schools students.

SIMON AND GARFUNKEL'S "HOMEWARD BOUND" is playing on the tape deck. It is after midnight and I have just gotten into a car with three strangers at the Sioux Falls airport. We are fifty miles from Brookings on I–29. I speak quietly with the driver. The other two passengers speak more quickly to one another in Tamil. All three are electrical engineers from India, studying at SDSU, where my father taught for many years. Fifteen miles out, I turn to the woman from Madras who has never been on this straight black road before, never seen such open space, and say, "Those are the lights of Brookings. You won't be able to see them again for awhile, but they are there. I grew up on this road."

Shortly before 2 A.M., I will ask to be dropped off near Brookings High School. I want to walk, I say, the few blocks to my family's place, to clear my head. The streets are completely silent, the air, even in early August, is sharp and clear. In the entryway of my parent's condo, I hesitate, then ring the buzzer once. I am immediately admitted, and say only: "I have a story."

The story started at 3:00 the afternoon before in Chicago's O'Hare. I have spent days of my life here, and want to see the long glass walkway again. I glance to the left, see a green sky and think, "That's odd. That looks like a pop-up storm. Chicago doesn't have those." Twenty minutes later, all ground and air traffic has stopped. Planes on the ground waiting to be unloaded are parked because the lightning makes it unsafe for anyone to be outside.

Back in the gate area, the flight to Syracuse is delayed because the plane from Sioux Falls is not on the ground yet. I have dealt with this before. I know that I will have plenty of time to find a Starbucks stand, a *New York Times*, and a book on *How to be a Great Boss* that I would not be seen with anywhere else. Ever. In a seat next to me, I notice a young woman with skin darker than mine, although not by much, flipping through the pages of her passport. In another seat close, someone clearly dressed for Syracuse. None of this is unusual. I have one foot in the generation that still dressed up for flights. Blazer, hose, matching purse and case, jewelry from my friend Carolyn that matches my blazer, neck pillow. It is not unusual for other women traveling alone to sit next to me. I look (and am) safe, and they can sense it.

She started in Madras thirty hours ago, transferred through Frankfurt, cleared customs in Chicago. She thinks she is two hours away from landing in South Dakota. She will be studying at SDSU in the masters program to be an electrical engineer. She has never been stateside before. The language of instruction in Madras is English. I tell her not to worry about the delay to Syracuse—it isn't our plane. I tell her that I am not an expert, but that I always went to school far away from home. The woman who is actually flying to Syracuse, almost certainly another academic, listens politely, smiles, and then drifts away. Before long, the flight to Syracuse is canceled.

When the flight to Sioux Falls is canceled, I tell the agent at the gate: "We didn't start together, but we are traveling together now." He books us both standby on the next flight (already delayed), my ticket more quickly because it is electronic. Looking at her paper ticket, he says "The only thing I can tell you is don't lose that ticket." I offer the use of my cell phone. Every hour or so, she calls her friends in Brookings, or they call her. She sleeps, not enough. She cries a little, and I can say nothing to help.

A rumor moves through the gate area that the standby list goes by the number of frequent flyer miles. I know that means I will be on the flight, and she will not. I don't tell her that. I do explain that we can't take a cab for the 600 miles from Chicago to our town on the northern high plains. I know that it is time to buy another neck pillow, another water bottle, and something to eat. I ask if she has any dietary restrictions. She is a vegetarian. I prepare to spend the night in O'Hare.

After 10:30, when the flight is finally boarding, the first name called on the standby list is mine. I put my hand on her shoulder and say, "Not yet." In front of us, a very angry young woman and a very drunk young man are complaining about how long they have been waiting.

The process stops for ten minutes before the list of names resumes. She says, "Don't leave me" and then "Pray for me." When the last name has been called, I am still standing near the door with a boarding pass and a matching blazer. There are still seats available, but the crew has run out of time for boarding. Suddenly, an agent notices me and says, "Wait a minute, did she volunteer?" Politely and quietly I say, "I am not getting on the plane without her." I look around at two gate agents who have worked too long, and three yellow-slickered runway workers who have been out all day in the rain. Together, the agents decide to print the last boarding pass of the day. And suddenly, we are all smiling. We will be home late, but we will be home.

There is quiet applause on the plane, one or two people (who have been following the story and wishing her well) say "Welcome to South Dakota." When we are in the air, I deliver her water bottle back and say, "Yes, I did reach your friends. They will be meeting us."

Notes:

Notes:

Notes:

Notes: